British Racing Green

British Racing Green

Drivers, Cars and Triumphs of British Motor Racing

David Venables

Series Editor: Karl Ludvigsen

Ian Allan
PUBLISHING

David Venables

Karl Ludvigsen

David Venables - Author

Formerly the Official Solicitor, David Venables is the Assistant Editor of the Vintage Sports Car Club Bulletin and a regular contributor to *The Automobile*. He is the author of motor racing histories on 1930s *voiturette* racing Napier, Bugatti and Alfa Romeo and also the *Official Centenary History of Brooklands*. He lives in Sussex and is a keen vintage motorist, driving a 1930 Aston Martin and a 1936 Fiat.

Karl Ludvigsen – Series Editor

In addition to his motor industry activities as an executive (with GM, Fiat and Ford) and head of a consulting company, Karl Ludvigsen has been active for over 50 years as an author and historian. As an author, co-author or editor he has some fifty books to his credit – all of them about cars and the motor industry, Karl's life long passion.

Since 1997 Ludvigsen has been drawing on the photographic resources of the Ludvigsen Library to write and illustrate books on the great racing drivers, including Stirling Moss, Jackie Stewart, Juan Manuel Fangio, Dan Gurney, Alberto Ascari, Bruce McLaren, and Emerson Fittipaldi.

He has written about road racing in America, the cars of the Can-Am series, the AAR Eagle racing cars, the GT40 Fords and *Prime Movers*, the story of Britain's Ilmor Engineering.

His introduction to *At Speed*, a book of Jesse Alexander's racing photography, won the Ken W. Purdy Award for Excellence in Automotive Journalism. He has written three times about Mercedes-Benz, twice about its racing cars. His books on the latter subject have won the Montagu Trophy (once) and the Nicholas-Joseph Cugnot Award (twice), both recognising outstanding automotive historical writing. In 2001 he again received the Cugnot award from the Society of Automotive Historians for his book about the early years of the Volkswagen, *Battle for the Beetle*. In 2002 the Society gave him its highest accolade, Friend of Automotive History.

Resident in England since 1980, Mr Ludvigsen is respected as a close and knowledgeable observer of, and participant in, the world motor industry. On motor industry topics Karl Ludvigsen has written books about high-performance engines, the Wankel rotary engine, the histories of American auto makers and the V12 Engine.

He is a former technical editor of *Sports Cars Illustrated* (1956-57), editor of *Car and Driver* (1960-1962) and east coast editor of *Motor Trend* (1970s). His articles have been published in America by *Road & Track* and *Automobile Quarterly*, among others, while in Europe he writes frequently for *The Automobile*. He is a columnist for *Hemmings Sports & Exotic Cars* and Just-Auto.com and a senior writer for Autosport-Atlas.com, a leading motor racing website.

British Racing Green © 2008

ISBN (13) 978 0 71110 3332 0

Produced by Chevron Publishing Limited
Concept: Robert Forsyth
Project Editors: Robert Forsyth/Chevron Publishing
and Karl Ludvigsen
Cover and book design: Mark Nelson
© Text: David Venables
© Colour profiles: Steve Anderson

Published by Ian Allan Publishing
an imprint of Ian Allan Publishing Ltd, Hersham, Surrey KT12 4RG.

Printed by Ian Allan Printing Ltd, Hersham, Surrey KT12 4RG.

Visit the Ian Allan Publishing website at:
www.ianallanpublishing.com

Ian Allan
PUBLISHING

CONTENTS

FOREWORD

This book, one of an unique series from Ian Allan Publishing, was conceived to introduce the reader to the cars, circuits, companies and characters of one of the great motor sporting nations. Soon after the first races of 1895 the issue of nationality loomed large in Europe, birthplace of motoring. In fact the first major international motor race, the Gordon Bennett Cup of 1900 to 1905, was contested not by companies but by trios of cars representing their nations. Every part of every car had to be manufactured in the respective countries.

By the 1920s cars from France, Germany, Great Britain, the United States, Italy and Austria were prominent in international motor sports, distinguished by their official national colours. With the rebirth of assertive nationalism in the 1930s their colours took on new significance as the flag-bearers of European nations took to the tracks to demonstrate their skills and superiority.

After World War Two their colours bespoke the nationality of racing cars until the late 1960s, when liveries were allowed to reflect sponsorship. Though this relaxation of constraints did produce fabulous looking racing cars, some competitors continued to reflect their countries of construction in their choice of colours. Because national identities are blurred when French racing cars are made in Britain and German cars are produced in Switzerland — as they are in the 21st Century — the new paradigm can be seen to have its merits.

Introduced, explained and illustrated in these pages are the companies, engineers, executives and enthusiasts whose powerful competitive spirit and dauntless courage drove them to dominate in motor racing. A leading expert reveals the dramatic stories behind their successes and failures in the great classic endurance races and Grand Prix contests in which they dominated — or faced disaster. Motor racing, which has no equal in the ecstasy of victory and agony of defeat, comes vividly to life in this volume's colourful pages.

Karl Ludvigsen
Series Editor

MANUFACTURERS:

1. Napier: London SE1 (South Bank) and Acton, London W3

2. Sunbeam: Wolverhampton

3. Bentley: Cricklewood, London NW2 and Derby

4. MG: Abingdon

5. ERA: Bourne, Lincs

6. Aston Martin: Feltham, Middx and Newport Pagnell

7. Lagonda: Staines, Middx

8. Riley: Coventry

9. Austin: Longbridge, Birmingham

10. Alta and HRG: Tolworth, Surrey

11. HWM: Walton-on-Thames, Surrey

12. Connaught: Ripley, Surrey

13. BRM: Bourne, Lincs

14. Vanwall: Park Royal, London W3

15. Cooper: Surbiton, Surrey

16. Jaguar: Coventry

17. Lotus: Cheshunt, Herts and Hethel, Norfolk

18. Brabham: Byfleet, Surrey

19. Tyrrell: Ockham, Surrey

20. Lola: Huntingdon

21. Williams: Didcot

22. McLaren: Woking

23. Alvis: Coventry

24. Lea Francis: Coventry

25. Talbot: London W10

26. Frazer Nash: Isleworth, Middx

27. Morgan: Malvern

28. Reynard: Bicester

29. AC: Thames Ditton

30. Invicta: Cobham

CIRCUITS & TRACKS:

31. Brooklands Weybridge, Surrey

32. Shelsley Walsh, Worcestershire

33. Donington Park, Derbyshire

34. Silverstone, Northants

35. Goodwood, Chichester, Sussex

36. Aintree, Merseyside

37. Isle of Man

38. Ards, Northern Ireland

39. Dundrod, Northern Ireland

UK manufacturing sites of racing cars – past and present and the racing circuits and tracks used

CHAPTER I

All a Matter of Colour

THE phrase 'British Racing Green' conjures up images of Bentleys and Jaguars at Le Mans, Coopers, Vanwalls and Lotuses in Grands Prix and countless British cars in motor races through the decades. Thus one might think that British cars raced in green from the earliest days until commercial liveries took the stage in the late 1960s. Some green cars are still racing in the 21st century. Even under the multi-coloured sponsored liveries, the 'BRG' spirit still lives on. But the real story of British green is much less straightforward.

The beginnings of national racing colours were convoluted and muddled. The first motor race was run from Paris to Rouen in 1894, and the sport soon grew in the remaining years of the 19th century. Almost all the races were from city-to-city, mostly starting or finishing in Paris. The sport was organised by the French and most of the cars and drivers were French, so there was little international competition, but all this changed in 1900.

With the aim of encouraging the development of the car, James Gordon-Bennett, the proprietor of the New York Herald, offered the Automobile Club de France a challenge trophy which was to be contested annually between the national automobile clubs of the various countries. But there was a stipulation that every part of the competing cars had to be made in the country which they represented. The 1900 Gordon Bennett Trophy attracted entries from France, the United States, Germany and Belgium. The organisers decreed that the cars of each team should be painted in a distinctive colour. The French cars should be painted blue, the American red, the German white and the Belgian yellow.

There was no British participation. Motoring was being accepted grudgingly in the UK. Racing on public roads was strictly forbidden, so racing had little support. The first British participation in an international motor race took place on 25 July 1900, six weeks after the first Gordon Bennett competition, when S.F. Edge drove an H70 Napier in the Paris-Toulouse-Paris race. He retired after a mere 50 miles (80 kms) with ignition failure. The colour of that Napier has been forgotten but a great and indeed heroic story had begun.

When the Gordon Bennett was run again in May 1901 there seem to have been no stipulations about the colour of the cars. This time there was a British entry with Edge driving a Napier, a monstrous machine with a 16-litre engine, which was painted red. The race was run between Paris and Bordeaux and Edge dropped out near Poitiers with a broken clutch. He was back in France at the end of June when he drove the Napier 'Monster' in the Paris-

The first green car. Charles Jarrott in his Panhard at Aachen during the 1901 Paris-Berlin race.

CHARLES JARROTT

If being the first to race a green car were not sufficient, Charles Jarrott had another distinction as a racing pioneer. He took part in the first motor race in Britain. This was held for motor tricycles on a cycle track at Sheen House on the south-west outskirts of London in November 1897. As well, Jarrott won the first race for cars in Britain, coming first with a Panhard in a one-mile contest on Crystal Palace's cycle velodrome in April 1901.

In the wider world he raced his green Panhard in the 1901 Paris-Berlin race, then was victorious in the 1902 Circuit des Ardennes in Belgium. He goes into the record book as the first Briton to win an international circuit race.

The next year, 1903, Jarrott drove a De Dietrich to fourth place overall in the notorious Paris-Madrid, the last of the city-to-city open-road races, which was stopped at Bordeaux after the deaths of several drivers and spectators. After that he switched to a Napier, which he crashed in the 1903 Gordon Bennett, then took 14th place in the 1904 competition with a Wolseley.

For early motorists there was keen competition to hold the record for the fastest time from London to Monte Carlo. This was held twice by Jarrott in 1906 and 1907 with a Crossley. The opening meeting at Brooklands in 1907 saw him in action. He dead-heated for first place in a race driving a De Dietrich. After that his racing activities gradually tailed off. Jarrott died in 1944 aged 77. His fine classic book, *Ten Years of Motoring and Motor Racing*, was the first motor racing autobiography.

Berlin race. Also competing was the British driver Charles Jarrott who was highly regarded by the French for his driving skill and had been entered for the race by the French manufacturer Panhard et Levassor.

When Jarrott went to the Panhard factory in Paris before the race he found that his car had the race number 13, but it was explained to him that it had been painted green, regarded as a lucky colour in France, to invalidate the baleful effect of the unlucky number. The combination seemed to be effective as Jarrott finished in 10th place, despite an off-road excursion when his riding mechanic was thrown from the car.

The 1902 Gordon Bennett competition was run concurrently with the race from Paris to Vienna. Edge's Napier was one of the British entries, painted in an olive shade of green. It has been suggested that this was

The trials for the 1904 British Gordon Bennett team in the Isle of Man: (l to r) Earp (Napier), Muir (Wolseley), Edge (Napier), Girling (Wolseley) and Jarrott (Wolseley).

The Gordon Bennett Trophy.

influenced by Jarrott, but many of the production touring cars from the Napier factory were painted green and this may also have been a factor. Edge gained a famous victory and so the responsibility of organising the 1903 Gordon Bennett Trophy race fell to the Automobile Club of Great Britain and Ireland (soon to become the Royal Automobile Club).

Racing was banned in England and so the ACGBI chose a course in Ireland in County Kildare. Britain was represented by a team of three Napiers painted in emerald green, allegedly as courtesy to the Irish hosts, but Jarrott as a member of the Napier team may have been influential because he had won the 1902 Circuit des Ardennes in Belgium, driving a green Panhard. The regulations allocated green to the Napiers and the signs of a pattern for the future was being established. The winning Mercedes was white and the French and American teams were blue and red respectively.

The British team for the 1904 Gordon Bennett race in Germany comprised a Napier for Edge and two Wolseleys, one driven by Jarrott, and all were painted green although the race regulations said nothing about colours.

The last Gordon Bennett Trophy race was held in France in 1905. This time the team colours were stipulated and Britain was allocated green. That should have settled the matter, but times were changing and with pressure from manufacturers who wanted to race, the top echelon of racing moved from national teams to manufacturers' teams. When the first Grand Prix race, the G.P. de l'ACF (French G.P.), was held in 1906, the cars, entered by manufacturers, appeared in a motley selection of colours and the winning Renault was painted red.

For a variety of reasons, mostly commercial, Grand Prix racing was abandoned from 1908 until 1912, but in 1911 the French newspaper *L'Auto* organised a race for cars up to 3.0-litre capacity, the Coupe de L'Auto, which was held at Boulogne. This drew a big international entry and colours were allocated. From Britain, teams were

Jock Hancock (Vauxhall) at the 1912 Coupe de L'Auto.

entered by Sunbeam, Vauxhall, Calthorpe and Arrol-Johnston. Arrol-Johnston, which came from Scotland, was allocated green and the other three English-based teams were told to find pots of red paint.

The next year the Coupe de L'Auto was run concurrently with the revived French G.P. and the Sunbeams were green, while the Arrol-Johnston team – perhaps in an early fit of nationalistic fervour of which Jackie Stewart would have approved – painted their cars in a tartan scheme. In 1913 the Sunbeams ran in the full French G.P. at Amiens in July, painted green, but red paint came out again for both Sunbeam and Vauxhall teams which competed in the *voiturette* Coupe de L'Auto at Boulogne, two months later.

In the legendary French G.P. of 1914, the last major motor race before Europe and the rest of the world hurtled headlong into World War One, the Sunbeam and Vauxhall teams were back in green again. All this seems to show that until 1914, while there was a strong preference or direction to green, Britain's national colour was still fluctuating between green and red.

Motor racing took some time to make a full recovery from the chaos of the war years and Grand Prix racing was not resumed until 1921 when the French G.P. was run at Le Mans. It seems that national racing colours had been settled and have remained unchanged since then. The Sunbeam team was painted green for this and subsequent races. When other British teams, notably Bentley, appeared on the racing scene during the 1920s, all were painted in various shades of green.

It was different in the world of record breaking. When Sunbeam broke the World Land Speed Record in 1926 and 1927, its cars were red. Malcolm Campbell, an arch-patriot, painted his series of 'Blue Bird' record breakers an appropriate blue, the 'Golden Arrow' of 1929 spoke for itself while the 'Thunderbolt' of George Eyston and the Railton of John Cobb, both Land Speed Record holders in the 1930s, were silver.

When the political tensions of the 1930s brought a great surge of nationalism, racing colours gained a new significance, especially for the German, Italian and French teams. While factory teams always adopted their national colours, private entrants in Grand Prix racing had more latitude. They would either race in their national colour, or the colour of their car's origin, or sometimes adopt a personal colour.

For the lesser *voiturette* class and for sports cars there were no rules. The British entrants in these classes had no outright preference for green. The ERA team sometimes raced in green but also ran in black and their private entrants used whatever colour pleased them. In sports car racing the Aston Martin team ran in red; in 1935 a red-painted Lagonda won the Le Mans 24-hour race.

With the end of World War Two it seemed that British drivers would again race in green cars, but in the autumn of 1946 the Royal Automobile Club (RAC) proposed that the national colour should be changed to blue. This was submitted to the Federation International de l'Automobile (FIA), the international governing body of motor racing. To differentiate from blue French cars, the British blue would be distinguished by a Union Jack of 1,575 square centimetres on both sides of the car.

There was a huge outcry from British competitors and enthusiasts. The motoring press was bombarded with letters of outrage. After two months of angry debate and protest, in December 1946 the RAC admitted that it had been misguided and it was agreed that green would continue to be the British racing colour.

For the next 20 years green cars gained huge prestige by dominating all aspects of motor racing, but the influence of commercial sponsors of the sport was growing. In 1968 commercial advertising was permitted on cars for the first time. Immediately teams took the opportunity to paint their cars with a complete commercial livery and green cars soon became a rare sight in top-line racing.

There were rare exceptions. The Jaguar Formula 1 team, albeit owned by Ford, raced green cars from 2000 to 2004 and, in 2003, a green Bentley was victorious at

Le Mans – though this had an element of irony, as it was owned and built by very German Audi.

With the globalisation of motor racing it is now difficult to ascribe a definite nationality to a car. Many cars with a foreign identity are built in England and British cars frequently have foreign power units. When a British-built and -powered car wins an international race, though, there is still a surge of pride which echoes the feelings of the past when the cars were painted green.

There have been many misconceptions about the shade of the colour which is British Racing Green. The answer is that there is no particular shade, though manufacturers sell new cars in a middling to dark shade of green which are catalogued as 'British Racing Green' and paint is sold of the same hue with that title.

The colour has varied with different cars over the past century. Napier and Sunbeam favoured a dark colour. Bentley seem, from recent research, to have used an olive colour while the works ERAs of the 1930s were often a pale apple shade, which was carried through to the first BRMs. A metallic green was favoured by the HWM team in the early 1950s and this was used by Aston Martin in sports car racing during that decade, culminating in a victory at Le Mans in 1959. So any shade will do as long as it is green.

Wyse in his tartan-painted Arrol-Johnston at the 1912 Coupe de L'Auto.

George Eyston's 'Thunderbolt' which held the World Land Speed Record at 357.50 mph in 1938.

CHAPTER 2

Napier: First to Wear the Green

S F. (Selwyn Francis) Edge was born in New South Wales, Australia in 1868; his parents were British and they returned to England in 1871. In his teens Edge became a keen racing cyclist. In 1896 he began racing motor tricycles in some of the earliest events in England, run at the Crystal Palace and at Sheen House, near Richmond. In 1898 he bought the Panhard which had won the Paris-Marseilles-Paris race in 1896.

Edge made some improvements to the Panhard and approached a fellow cycle racer, Montague Napier, who was the proprietor of an engineering company, D. Napier & Son, on a site where the Royal Festival Hall now stands on the south bank of the River Thames in London. Napier was commissioned to convert the steering from tiller to wheel operation.

Napier had designed a car which Edge considered was crude and poorly designed, so under Edge's guidance a new car was designed and built with a two-cylinder 2,471 cc engine. Edge drove this in the 1900 1,000-Mile Trial which ran from London to Edinburgh and back again, passing through many major cities en route. This first Napier won its class and came second overall in the Trial. Encouraged by this success, Napier began building cars, with Edge as the sales agent.

Napier had designed a new car, the H70, with a four-cylinder engine. Edge, who wanted to compete in the 1901 Gordon Bennett Trophy, entered the first of these in the Paris-Toulouse-Paris race in July 1900 to gain valuable experience. He took the Hon. Charles Rolls (later of Rolls-Royce fame) as his riding mechanic, but the venture was unsuccessful and the Napier retired with ignition failure, though it was an historic landmark as the first time a British car had competed in an international race.

Edge studied the competition and concluded that he needed a car with great power for the Gordon Bennett contest. Napier designed a crude machine with a four-cylinder 16.3-litre engine which was known as the 'Monster'. In 1902 the Gordon Bennett was run concurrently with the Paris-Bordeaux race, but the red-painted Napier was excluded from the Gordon Bennett. Its English-made tyres were not up to the task and were replaced with French tyres, so the car failed to comply with the regulation that every part had to be made in its country of origin. It was allowed to run in the Paris-Bordeaux, but retired after two-thirds of the course with a broken clutch.

Napier went back to his drawing board and came up with a new design for the 1902 Gordon Bennett, the D50, with a four-cylinder engine of 6,436 cc. It was entered for the Gordon Bennett which ran concurrently with the Paris-Vienna race, although the Gordon Bennett competitors only had to race as far as Innsbruck. With the moustachioed Edge at its wheel the green Napier battled through to Innsbruck and was the winner.

Edge encountered many problems en route, but these were perhaps enhanced by him – including the dubious claim that he had changed tyres by removing these from the rims with his bare hands – to give his drive a truly heroic image. Despite the hyperbole, he had gained a great victory with the first British car to win an international contest and had also established Napier as one of the leading English manufacturers.

Because a British car had won the 1902 race, the honour of organising the 1903 Gordon Bennett contest fell to the Automobile Club of Great Britain & Ireland (later the RAC), but as racing on public roads was forbidden in England, it was run over a circuit in County Kildare, Ireland. A team of three Napiers represented Great Britain. Two were the E61 model, a development of the 1902 winner, but the third was a new design, the K5 with a 13.7-litre engine.

The K5 was driven by Edge and the three cars were painted in an emerald shade of green, as a compliment to the Irish hosts. Subsequently, after the factory was moved to Acton in West London, racing Napiers were painted in a darker green, with the same paint used for the doors and windows of the factory and collected from the works stores when needed.

The race was a Napier failure, both E61s crashing and Edge finishing last in the K5, having been delayed by tyre failures and overheating. At the end of 1903 Napier broke new ground with the design of a six-cylinder engine. This was not ready for the eliminating trials run on the Isle of Man by the RAC to select the British team for the 1904 Gordon Bennett. The ACGBI chose Edge in a K5 Napier and two Wolseleys driven by Charles Jarrott and Sidney Girling.

Although Napier's six-cylinder L48 was ready in time for the race which was held at Homburg, in Germany, the ACGBI decreed that as it had not participated in the trials it could not be in the team, much to Edge's disgust and annoyance. The race was over four laps of an 80 mile circuit; Edge drove the K5 and retired after three laps with overheating, while Girling was ninth and Jarrott was eleventh.

In January 1905 the L48 was taken to the United States to compete in the Florida Speed Week, which was held on the long, straight and hard beach at Daytona near

Miami. Driven by Arthur Macdonald, a works test driver, it ran in the flying-mile competition and set a new Land Speed Record of 104.65 mph. Although there was some dispute between the AIACR (Alliance Internationale des Automobile Clubs Reconnus – this was the governing body for world motor sport before World War Two) and the American Automobile Association about the methods of timing, nevertheless the L48 was the fastest car in the world, though its record did not stand for long. Despite its speed, the L48 failed to make an impression when run in the 1905 Gordon Bennett race as it was delayed by carburettor problems and finished ninth.

For the rest of the 1905 season and throughout 1906, Napier's racing activity was low-key, but in 1907 the Brooklands track was opened. This was the world's first purpose-built motor-racing course and the only venue where continuous high speed could be maintained. Edge booked the track as soon as it was formally opened in June 1907 for an attempt on the world 24-hour record. His aim was to run a team of three production T21 Napiers at an average speed of a mile a minute for the 24 hours.

The attempt was a triumph as the three cars completed the run with virtually no problems and all exceeded the target speed Edge had set. The car driven by Edge covered the greatest distance, 1,581 miles at an average of 65.9 mph . When racing began at Brooklands

S.F. Edge and the H70 Napier, which he drove in the 1900 Paris-Toulouse-Paris race. It was the first British car to compete in an international race.

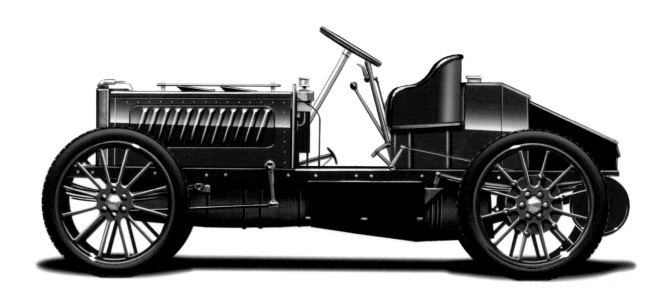

1902 D50 Napier

The 6.4-litre D50 Napier was the first British car to score an international victory, with success in the 1902 Gordon Bennett Trophy race. S.F. Edge with his cousin Cecil Edge as his riding mechanic, was the only finisher in the race which ran over open roads from Paris to Innsbruck via Belfort and Bregenz.

in July 1907, Napiers were dominant. A Napier driven by Frank Newton tied in a dead heat for victory in the very first race with a Lorraine-Dietrich driven by Jarrott and the success continued for the rest of the season. There was controversy, as Napier was using an oxygen cylinder whose contents were vented into the carburettor to gain extra power in a close finish. The success of this ruse soon resulted in a ban on the practice.

In 1908 Napier built a team of cars for the French Grand Prix. This had taken the place of the Gordon Bennett race in 1906 and was a race between manufacturers instead of national teams. The Napiers were fitted with quick-release Rudge Whitworth wire wheels, but these were declared to be illegal by the race organisers. An affronted Edge withdrew the team from the race, expressing much publicised outrage and declaring the ban to be prompted by French chauvinism.

At Brooklands the success continued though there was a setback when the L48 failed in a highly publicised match race with a Fiat at the Whitsun meeting. In 1905 the RAC had initiated the Tourist Trophy which was run on a road

circuit on the Isle of Man, much of which is still used for the motorcycle TT. A Napier team was unsuccessful in 1905 when the victory went to a Rolls-Royce.

Napier ignored the race in 1906 and 1907, provoking widespread comment that Edge was unwilling to face the possibility of defeat. The 1908 Tourist Trophy was restricted to four-cylinder cars and Napier was committed to making six-cylinder cars, and so for the race a team of four-cylinder cars was built at the Acton factory, ostensibly under contract for a new manufacturer, Ernest Hutton. If the cars succeeded, the Napier origin would be admitted, if they failed, it would be ascribed to Hutton. The gamble was successful and a Hutton won the race, driven by William Watson. Soon after the race Hutton announced that he had decided not to continue with the manufacture of cars!

Edge and Montague Napier realised that racing was expensive and that to benefit from publicity the successes had to be maintained. Using the pretext that the company could gain nothing more from racing and that racing, following some fatal accidents at Brooklands, was

S.F. Edge waits for the start in the 1903 Gordon Bennett Trophy with his K5 Napier. The width and primitive condition of the road are noticeable.

Clifford Earp in the L48 Napier during the 1905 Gordon Bennett Trophy, held at Clermont Ferrand. He finished ninth after fuel and carburettor problems. The L48 held the World Land Speed Record briefly in 1905.

Edge before the start of his 24-hour record run at Brooklands in 1907. The windscreen collapsed during the last hour.

NAPIER

dangerous and undesirable, Napier announced in September 1908 that it was pulling out of the sport. That seemed to be the end of Napier's glory in motor racing and Edge and Napier subsequently parted acrimoniously.

The firm continued to make production cars and commercial vehicles until the outbreak of World War One in 1914. During the war the company built aero engines under licence from other manufacturers, but in 1916 Arthur Rowledge, who had become chief designer, produced the Lion, a 12-cylinder engine laid out in three banks of four to make a broad arrow. The Lion went into production too late to take any part in the war, but in the 1920s it became a standard engine for use by the Royal Air Force.

In the 1920s there was intense competition to gain the Land Speed Record with the holders of the record becoming popular heroes. Malcolm Campbell built a record contender and persuaded Napier to let him have a Lion to power it. In February 1927 his 'Blue Bird' set a new record of 174.88 mph on Pendine Sands in Carmarthenshire, Wales. A year later, a rebuilt and improved 'Blue Bird' set a new record of 206.95 mph at Daytona Beach in Florida.

Meanwhile for Henry Segrave, who had broken Campbell's record in 1927 with a Sunbeam, Capt. J.S. 'Jack' Irving built a car, the 'Golden Arrow' which also used a Lion engine. With this Segrave raised the record to 231.44 mph at Daytona in March 1929. Not to be outdone, Campbell returned to the fray in February 1931. 'Blue Bird' was a new car powered by a Lion which had been modified and highly tuned for the Schneider Trophy air race. Going back to Daytona, Campbell set a new record of 245.73 mph. Returning to Daytona 12 months later, Campbell and 'Blue Bird' broke their own record, pushing it up to 253.97 mph.

That seemed to be the end of Napier's glory as Campbell abandoned the Lion and turned to Rolls-Royce

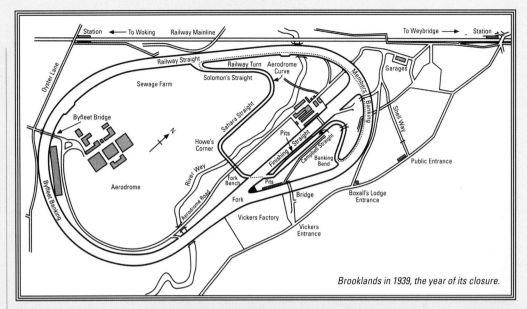

Brooklands in 1939, the year of its closure.

Brooklands was the inspired creation of one man. Hugh Locke-King was a rich landowner who built the track at Weybridge, on the south-western outskirts of London. It was the first purpose-built motor course in the world. With its huge concrete bankings, the cost of the pear-shaped 2.76-mile track almost bankrupted him. Opened in 1907, Brooklands was designed for a maximum speed of 120 mph. Deservedly it became the centre of British motor sport, staging races for cars and motorcycles. It was also used by manufacturers for testing and record runs.

The Brooklands infield became one of the first British airfields. From 1909 it was home to the embryonic British aircraft industry, attracting many companies, notably Vickers. During World War One Brooklands was a major centre of aircraft production with Vickers building a large factory adjoining the southern edge of the track.

After racing resumed in 1920, throughout the 1920s and 1930s meetings were held almost every weekend from March until October. It was the scene of major long-distance races. The British Grand Prix was held there in 1926 and 1927. Brooklands hosted important sports car races and the BRDC 500-mile race was for many years, the fastest long-distance contest in the World.

By the 1930s the track, increasingly dated, was at risk of becoming a motor-racing backwater. In an attempt to improve it an artificial road circuit was opened in 1937. Brooklands closed in 1939 when World War Two began and the Vickers factory expanded across the track. Once again it became a centre of aircraft production. Almost all the Hawker Hurricanes which fought in the Battle of Britain were built there.

Too badly damaged to be repaired at the end of the war, Brooklands was sold to Vickers who continued to expand. Many famous aircraft were built there including substantial parts of Concorde. When aircraft production finished in the 1970s parts of the track were sold off for commercial development, but many original buildings and substantial parts of the banking have been preserved to form the centre of the Brooklands Museum. Although there is no racing, the Museum holds motoring events throughout the year.

Henry Segrave seated in the Irving-Napier 'Golden Arrow' at Daytona in 1929.

NAPIER

John Cobb has a push start in the Napier-Railton at Brooklands. This car holds the outright Brooklands lap record for all time and also held the World One-Hour and 24-Hour records in 1936.

JOHN COBB

John Cobb, the fastest man ever to lap the Brooklands track, also had the distinction of holding the World Land Speed Record continuously for 23 years. A quiet and modest man, Cobb made his living as a fur broker. He started racing at Brooklands in the 1920s. He had a passion for big cars. His first record-breaker was a 10-litre Delage which had held the Land Speed Record in 1923. Cobb raced this at Brooklands and set a lap record of 132.11 mph In 1933 he had built the Napier-Railton, the fastest car yet seen at the track. With it Cobb set the ultimate lap record at 143.44 mph (230.83 km/h) in 1935, also winning a clutch of races, the fastest ever run at Brooklands. The next year the Napier-Railton went to the Bonneville Salt Flats in Utah and took the World One-Hour and

24-Hour records. Cobb was still not satisfied. He commissioned the Napier-engined Railton land-speed-record car. Back at Bonneville he pushed the world record up to 369.75 mph (595.03 km/h) in 1939. Then World War Two intervened.

Dusted down after the war, the Railton went back to Bonneville in 1947. This time John Cobb set the record at 394.16 mph, achieving over 400 mph on one run. His record stood until 1964. Cobb wanted to be the fastest man on water as well as land. In 1952 he took his jet-powered boat, 'Crusader', to Loch Ness. On its first run 'Crusader' exceeded 200 mph (320 km/h), easily breaking the existing record, but on the return run the boat broke up and the gallant, modest 53-year-old Cobb was killed.

for a new engine for 'Blue Bird', but the story had a fresh twist. John Cobb was a keen and successful competitor at Brooklands who had held the lap record for the track in 1929 with a V-12 Delage. He wanted a car which would be suitable for racing at the track and could also take long-distance records.

Cobb commissioned the brilliant Reid Railton to design a car, the Napier-Railton, around a Lion engine. Built by Thomson & Taylor, the Brooklands tuners and engineers, it was immediately successful when it first appeared at Brooklands in 1933. With it Cobb broke the Brooklands outright lap record several times, finally setting it for all time at 143.44 mph in 1935.

The Napier-Railton was also successful in competition at Brooklands. As well as shorter races, it won the BRDC 500-mile race, the fastest race in the world at that time, in 1935 and 1937. Cobb's aim that the car should take records was fulfilled when it took the world's 24-hour record at Bonneville, Utah in September 1936 at 150.16 mph as well as the world hour record at 167.69 mph.

The modest Cobb had grander ambitions. He wanted to hold the World Land Speed Record. He commissioned Railton to design a remarkable car. This had two 1,400 bhp Lion engines mounted on each side of an S-shaped backbone frame; one drove the front wheels and the other the rear wheels, while the driver sat ahead of the front axle.

This teardrop-shaped car, the Railton, was taken to Bonneville in September 1938 and promptly broke the record at 350.20 mph. George Eyston was at Bonneville with his twin-Rolls-Royce-powered record car 'Thunderbolt' and retook the record the following day. Cobb returned to Bonneville in August 1939, with World War Two looming, and pushed the record up to 369.23 mph.

In August 1947 John Cobb took his car – now known as the Railton-Mobil Special – back to Bonneville and in a final magnificent effort set the record at 394.19 mph with one run at 403 mph. Cobb's record stood until 1963,

and so Napier's influence and activity in motor racing and record breaking covered a span of 63 years.

Malcolm Campbell in his Napier-powered 'Blue Bird' in 1931.

John Cobb's Railton which held the World Land Speed Record from 1939 until 1963.

CHAPTER 3

Sunbeam: Grand Prix Pioneers

IRONICALLY a Frenchman was responsible for the first successful British Grand Prix contender. Louis Coatalen was born in France in 1879. He trained as an engineer and came to England in 1900. After working for Humber and Hillman, he joined Sunbeam in 1909 as chief engineer.

Sunbeam had been making solid cars with little sporting pretensions, but Coatalen soon changed this. He saw that racing was the best way of gaining publicity and improving production cars by development. His first racing venture was a 4.2-litre single-seater Sunbeam 'Nautilis' which he raced at Brooklands in 1910. Fast, winning several races at the track, it was notable for its bodywork which was an early study in aerodynamics.

In 1911 came Sunbeam's first entry in an international motor race, with a car in the Coupe de L'Auto, a race for 3.0-litre *voiturettes* at Boulogne. This was a virtually standard side-valve 12/16 hp Sunbeam, which went well until it retired after a minor crash. Encouraged by this, Coatalen prepared a team of three cars for the 1912 Coupe de L'Auto which was run at Dieppe, concurrently with the French Grand Prix. These also used the 12/16 hp engine, but were remarkably quick.

The 1912 race was run over two days. Each day the cars had to cover 10 laps of a 47-mile circuit. At the end of the second day the Sunbeams had swept the board in the *voiturette* Coupe de L'Auto, taking the first three places in a field of 33 starters. Even more meritoriously they had taken third, fourth and fifth places in the Grand Prix overall, defeating all but two of the fourteen starters. On their return to England Coatalen and his drivers, Victor Rigal, Dario Resta and Emil Medinger, were feted at a lunch given by the RAC.

In 1913 Coatalen persevered with his production-based side-valve engines. Although the cars came third in the Coupe de L'Auto at Boulogne and in the French Grand Prix at Amiens, these had insufficient power. New ground was broken at Brooklands in 1913 with a V-12 car, 'Toodles V', which won races and broke records. It was the first car built in Europe and the second in the world to use this engine configuration.

After such a promising start with comparatively modest cars, Sunbeam now began to go racing seriously. In the 1913 Coupe de L'Auto the winner had been a Peugeot. Coatalen obtained one of these and studied it meticulously. Then for 1914 he produced a car which had much in common with the Peugeot design, with a twin-camshaft four-cylinder engine. This appeared with a capacity of 3.3 litres for the Tourist Trophy in the Isle of Man. Kenelm Lee Guinness of the brewing family, who

was later to make KLG sparking plugs, scored a convincing victory in the 600-mile race. Never fully explained was the painting of the team's cars purple for this race.

A month later, with engines enlarged to 4½ litres, the Sunbeam team was at Lyon for the French Grand Prix, but the pace of the Mercedes team was too hot and fifth by Dario Resta was the best that could be achieved.

Although World War One ended racing in Europe for five years, Sunbeams were still active in the United States which did not enter the conflict until 1917. Sunbeams first raced in the United States in 1913 when Albert Guyot drove 'Toodles IV', one of Coatalen's Brooklands cars, in the Indianapolis 500 and finished fourth, the first British car to race at the famous Brickyard. One of the 1913 GP cars came seventh in the 1914 Indianapolis 500 and a 1914 GP car ran at Indy in 1915, coming 10th.

The prestige of Indianapolis was already significant, so a car was built for the 1916 '500', despite the demands of war production at Sunbeam's Wolverhampton factory. Using a 4.9-litre engine in a 1914 GP chassis, it took fourth place. As well as the 500, Sunbeams gained wins and places in several lesser American races up to 1917.

Racing did not start again in Europe until 1920 when Sunbeam had a new driver, Henry Segrave, who had been a pilot in the Royal Flying Corps during the war. The company's activities were restricted to British events in 1920. A team of 3.0-litre cars was built for the revived French G.P. in 1921, but had no success.

Louis Coatalen in the 4.2-litre Sunbeam 'Nautilus' at Brooklands in 1910.

Although there had been no glory in France, it was a different story in England. A special 18-litre V-12 car, built for Brooklands racing and for record breaking, appeared on the track at the end of 1921. It won several races and in May 1922, making runs along the Brooklands Railway Straight in both directions, driven by Sir

Jean Chassagne in the 9-litre V-12 Sunbeam which took the World One-Hour record at Brooklands in 1913. This was the first European V-12 engine.

Algernon Guinness, the brother of Kenelm Lee Guinness, it broke the World Land Speed Record with an average of 133.75 mph. To make its record runs the Sunbeam had to make a complete lap of the track and on one lap, leading into the timed section, the V-12 broke the Brooklands lap record.

Swiss Ernest Henri, whose Peugeot design had been studied so closely in 1914, was engaged by Coatalen to design a 2.0-litre GP car, but this failed in the 1922 French G.P. at Strasbourg, where the pace of the victorious Fiats was too hot. One of the 1921 GP cars won the Tourist Trophy in the Isle of Man, driven by Jean Chassagne.

Coatalen had been so impressed by the speed of the Fiats at Strasbourg that he engaged the Fiat designers, Vincenzo Bertarione and Walter Becchia, to design a Sunbeam for the 1923 French G.P. Sneers that the new 2.0-litre Sunbeams were 'green Fiats' were unfair as the engine was virtually a new design and was fitted to an improved 1922 chassis. The outcome was triumph, with Segrave the winner. Sunbeam achieved immortality as the first British car to win a Grand Prix. Segrave was followed home in second place by Albert Divo.

In October 1923 Divo won the Spanish Grand Prix on a steeply banked track at Sitges, beating a team of very fast Millers, which on the banked oval were racing in their natural habitat. Coatalen could be satisfied that his Sunbeam was the most successful Grand Prix car in Europe.

The Bertarione/Becchia engine was refined and improved for 1924 with a major development: the fitting of a supercharger. The engine went into a new and lower chassis. The team went to the French G.P. at Lyon with every hope of repeating its 1923 success as the cars were the fastest in practice. The cars used Bosch magnetos. The night before the race, the Bosch representative persuaded the team to fit a new and improved magneto. The result was disastrous as all three cars misfired throughout the race and victory went to Alfa Romeo.

Consolation came in September 1924 when Segrave won the Spanish G.P. at San Sebastian. The win was clouded, as Kenelm Lee Guinness crashed his Sunbeam during the race and his mechanic, Barratt, was killed. Earlier in the month the team had received another blow when Dario Resta was killed at Brooklands while attempting short-distance records in a 2.0-litre GP car.

A 3.3-litre Sunbeam which won the 1914 Tourist Trophy in the Isle of Man. A team of similar cars with 4½-litre engines competed in the 1914 French Grand Prix.

The V-12 Land Speed Record car had been sold to Malcolm Campbell, who – the day before Segrave's Spanish win – raised the Land Speed Record to 146.16 mph on Pendine Sands.

In 1925 Sunbeam announced a 3.0-litre sports car with a six-cylinder twin-cam engine. One of these came second in the Le Mans 24-hour race in June, but in Grand Prix racing the results were not so good. Third place in the French G.P. was the best the team could manage. Campbell took his blue-painted V-12 to Pendine again in July 1925 and raised the Land Speed Record to 150.87

mph. Coatalen also had his eye on the record. In March 1926 a new 4.0-litre V-12 car was brought out with an engine which used components from the 2.0-litre GP sixes. Segrave took the impressive supercharged car to Southport Sands and raised the record to 152.33 mph.

In August 1920 Sunbeam had amalgamated with the French company Darracq, which had already bought the English manufacturer Talbot. Thus the STD combine had been formed. All the Grand Prix racing activities of the combine had been run by Sunbeam, though some Sunbeams had been badged as Talbot and

Josef Christaens took fourth place with this 4.9-litre Sunbeam in the 1916 Indianapolis 500.

Sir Henry Segrave

American-born Irishman Henry Segrave came to motor racing via service as a pilot in the World War One Royal Flying Corps. He started racing a 1914 GP Opel at Brooklands. Joining the Sunbeam works team in 1921, he soon became the lead driver for the Sunbeam-Talbot-Darracq combine.

Segrave's Grand Prix debut was not successful but he won the first long-distance race in England, the 1921 200 Miles at Brooklands. In 1923 he went to the top of the record book when he came first in the French G.P. in a Sunbeam, scoring the first British Grand Prix victory. He did it again in Spain in 1924. Meanwhile he was notching up regular wins in a 1.5-litre Talbot-Darracq *voiturette*.

In March 1926 Sunbeam chose him to drive a 4.0-litre V-12 world Land Speed Record car on Southport sands. Segrave set a figure of 152.33 mph. His interest in circuit racing was waning, although he won the 200-mile race for the third time in 1926. In

1927 Segrave went to Florida with Sunbeam's 1,000-horsepower twin-aero-engined monster. On Daytona Beach he was the first man to exceed 200 mph on land.

Henry Segrave was back at Daytona in 1929 with the Napier-engined 'Golden Arrow', an elegant, slim machine designed by Capt. J.S. Irving and funded by trade sponsorship. The 'Golden Arrow' pushed the Land Speed Record up to 231.44 mph. For this exploit Segrave was knighted, becoming Sir Henry. He took up power-boat racing and set his sights on the water speed record

Segrave set a new record at Venice in September 1929 in his boat 'Miss England', then went to Lake Windermere in June 1930 to improve on his record. He achieved it at a speed of 98.76 mph, but the boat capsized on a second run and he was killed.

Segrave's Sunbeam takes White House corner at Le Mans during the 1921 French Grand Prix. The contrast with the surface of a modern Grand Prix course is noticeable.

One of the victorious Sunbeam team which came first, second and fourth in the 1923 French Grand Prix at Tours. This was the fourth placed car driven by Kenelm Lee Guinness. The donkey seems to be the centre of some amusement – perhaps being used for towing purposes?

1923 SUNBEAM GP

WITH VICTORY IN THE 1923 FRENCH GRAND PRIX AT TOURS, HENRY SEGRAVE'S 2.0-LITRE SUNBEAM WAS THE FIRST BRITISH

CAR TO WIN A GRAND PRIX RACE. IT WAS A RESOUNDING VICTORY AS THE OTHER CARS IN THE WOLVERHAMPTON-BASED

SUNBEAM TEAM FINISHED IN SECOND AND FOURTH PLACE.

Darracq entries, notably in the 1921 French G.P.

At the beginning of 1926 a new Grand Prix formula was introduced with a capacity limit of 1,500 cc. With the 2.0-litre GP cars obsolete it was decided that STD's contenders for the new formula should be built by Darracq in Paris. Darracq had considerable experience in building small-engined racing cars, with its 1,500 cc *voiturettes* dominating the class from 1921 until 1925. When, later in 1926, Coatalen moved to Paris to supervise the Darracq operations, Sunbeam's racing programme began to decline.

There was one last triumph. A new Land Speed Record car was designed by Capt. J.S. Irving, powered by two Sunbeam Matabele aero engines mounted in front of, and behind, the dauntless driver. This car, known as the '1000hp Sunbeam', was taken to Daytona in Florida in March 1927 by Henry Segrave, who stumped up the high cost of the journey to America personally. He took the Land Speed Record to 203.79 mph. Like the 1926 record breaker, the car was painted red.

Thereafter Sunbeam's racing activities were restricted to events at Brooklands. The 3.0-litre sports cars did not run at Le Mans again, but one was victorious in the first long-distance sports car race at Brooklands, the 1927 Six-Hour race, driven by George Duller, who was equally successful as a horse racing jockey.

For the next three years the 4.0-litre V-12 Sunbeam was the car to beat at Brooklands. Driven by Kaye Don it won many races and broke the lap record four times, the last time in 1930, when it lapped the track at 137.58 mph. The 1924 2.0-litre GP cars also achieved many wins at the track. In September 1928, driving one of these cars, Mrs Jill Scott set a new ladies' lap record at 120.88 mph.

When in 1930 the racing department at the Wolverhampton factory was closed this was almost the end of the story, but there was a final fiasco. A new Land Speed Record contender was built using two special 24-litre V-12 engines mounted in tandem in front of the driver. This monstrous machine, 31 feet long and called

the 'Silver Bullet', was taken to Daytona in March 1930. A record attempt was made with Kaye Don as the driver, but the car was a disastrous flop, its best speed only 186 mph. The costly venture ended in recriminations among those involved.

In 1924, at the height of its racing glory, the STD combine had borrowed heavily to pay its bills. To cover this it issued 8% Guaranteed Notes repayable in 1934. When the notes matured there were no funds left to redeem them and so the combine went into receivership. Sunbeam, together with Talbot, was bought from the receiver by the Rootes Group.

The name 'Sunbeam' emerged again on race circuits in the 1960s when Rootes introduced its Sunbeam Alpine and Sunbeam Tiger. These appeared in some sports car events including Le Mans, but without much success; an Alpine won the Energy Index at Le Mans in 1961. These were but shadows of former glories, although the 2.0-litre Sunbeam Talbot 90 saloon achieved much success in rallies and won the 1955 Monte Carlo Rally. After Sunbeam's Grand Prix successes in 1923 and 1924, 33 years would elapse before another British victory in a major Grand Prix, a *Grande Epreuve*.

In 1924, Sunbeam used an improved version of the successful 1923 GP engine, but now supercharged, increasing the output from 108 bhp to 138 bhp. This went into a new, lower chassis. The 1924 GP Sunbeam was the fastest car on the circuits, but magneto problems prevented a repeat of the French G.P. win, although there was success in the 1924 Spanish G.P. There were subsequently many wins at Brooklands.

The V-12 Sunbeam at Pendine in 1924, when Malcom Campbell took the World Land Speed Record at 146.16 mph. Campbell waits by the wheel.

Albert Divo at Gaillon hill climb in 1927 with the 4.0-litre V-12 Sunbeam. Segrave took the World Land Speed Record with this car at Southport in 1926. It later held the Brooklands lap record. As part of the STD combine, for this event it has a Talbot badge.

Segrave in the twin-engined 1000 hp Sunbeam at Daytona in 1927 when he raised the World Land Speed Record to 203.79 mph.

Per Malling and Gunnar Fadum on their way to victory in the 1955 Monte Carlo Rally with their Sunbeam-Talbot 90.

CHAPTER 4

Bentley: The Cars, the Man and the Boys

Walter Owen Bentley
16 September 1888 - 3 August 1971

MORE glamour, aura and legend attaches to 'Bentley' than to any other marque in early British motor racing history. The progenitor of the marque, Walter Owen Bentley ('WO'), was born in 1888. When he left school in 1905 he became a premium apprentice with the Great Northern Railway. A premium apprentice was a relatively superior being because his parents paid the company a premium which was returned to him as wages during the five years of the apprenticeship. During his five years WO learned practical and theoretical engineering skills based on the company's locomotives. Unkind critics have said this influence showed in the cars he subsequently made.

During his apprenticeship WO began competing in motorcycle trials. Ambitiously he entered for a motorcycle race at Brooklands on Easter Monday 1909. He raced with some success there in 1909 and 1910 and also rode in the Isle of Man TT. In 1912 WO joined his brother, who had become the English importer of the French DFP car.

In 1913 WO drove a race-prepared DFP at Brooklands, improving its performance substantially by fitting aluminium pistons, helping to pioneer this development in England. He won a race at Brooklands and also broke class records at the track with the DFP and raced it in the Tourist Trophy in the Isle of Man in 1914. Although the smallest car in the race, the 2.0-litre DFP finished the two-day event in sixth place.

During World War One WO was commissioned into the Royal Naval Air Service and worked on aero engines, culminating in the production of his own designs, the Bentley Rotary BR1 and BR2. The engines were made in substantial numbers, the BR1 seeing service in the Sopwith Camel while the BR2 was fitted to the Sopwith Snipe.

At the end of the war WO formed Bentley Motors. Working with F.T. Burgess, who had designed the 1914 TT Humber, he commenced the design of a car of 3.0 litres. The first Bentley prototype was finished in January 1920. A factory was built at Cricklewood in North London, but development took longer than expected and the first car was not delivered to a customer until September 1921.

A second prototype, driven by Frank Clement, won its first race at the 1921 Whitsun meeting at Brooklands, but WO had greater ambitions. In 1922 a tuned production car was taken to Indianapolis for the 500-mile race. Although not fast enough to challenge for the lead, it made a great impression with a trouble free run and came 13th driven by Douglas Hawkes.

The revived Tourist Trophy was run in the Isle of Man in 1922, attracting a team of three Bentleys similar to the Indy car driven by Hawkes, Clement and WO. The cars went well in the 300-mile race, which was run in heavy rain, the drivers protected by makeshift plywood mud shields. They finished 2nd, 4th and 5th, taking the team prize.

A year later the first seeds were sown from which the legend grew. In 1923 the Le Mans 24-hour race was instituted and a 3.0-litre Bentley was entered by John Duff, a London agent for the marque. Driven by Duff and Clement it finished third, although it had led the race for a while until it was stopped by a punctured fuel tank. It only got going again after Clement had bicycled round the circuit with a can of fuel and mended the leak with chewing gum.

Duff and Clement returned to Le Mans in 1924. This time victory was secured, the Bentley finishing with a margin of 90 miles over the Lorraine in second place, gaining the first of six wins that would follow over the next 79 years. By 1925 Le Mans had become a major event. That year there were 49 starters, with two Bentleys which were official works entries. The race was a disaster with both cars dropping out. It was even worse in 1926, when two cars broke down and the third crashed.

After these Le Mans debacles, things looked black for Bentley Motors, but a saviour appeared in the guise of Woolf Barnato, the ebullient heir to a huge South African diamond and gold fortune. Barnato effectively bought Bentley Motors, leaving WO in charge of design and production. Already a keen competition driver, Barnato was eager for Bentley to continue racing. As well as funding the racing, Barnato was the inspiration behind the 'Bentley Boys', as the team drivers became known. Their social frolics in the late 1920s became almost as legendary as the exploits of the cars they drove.

The year 1927 saw the first long-distance sports car race at Brooklands, the Six-Hour race. Four works 3.0 litres were entered, one driven by Barnato and another by a new driver, Henry (Tim) Birkin. Though mechanical problems intervened, the Birkin car was third. The team went to Le Mans with mixed feelings, but the outcome was one of the all-time heroic drives that greatly enhanced the burgeoning Bentley legend.

The 1927 race was the debut of the new 4½-litre four, which was backed up by two 3.0-litre cars. The new car took an immediate lead. As darkness fell, the 4½ took White House corner to find the track blocked by a crashed Th. Schneider. It hit the stationary car and overturned. The 3.0 litre driven by George Duller crashed into their

Exp 1 – the 1921 prototype Bentley.

wrecks, only to be followed, as if drawn by a magnet, by the second 3.0 litre driven by Sammy Davis.

Davis managed to extract his badly damaged car. It was patched up in the pits, but it had only one headlamp and the front axle and frame were bent. Davis and Benjafield, his co-driver, rejoined the race, struggling on with damaged brakes and uncertain steering. An Aries led the race by six laps, but gradually the damaged Bentley cut this back. Although the Aries speeded up, under pressure from the Bentley its engine burst and with an hour to go the Bentley, soon to be known immortally as 'Old No.7', took the lead and went on to win.

The 3.0-litre Bentley which finished second in the 1922 Tourist Trophy. A similar car ran in the 1922 Indianapolis 500.

Both fortuitous and legendary, this victory marked a turning point in Bentley's racing fortunes. Backed by Barnato's funds, the team's efforts now went into the 4½ litre. Three ran in the Essex Six-Hour race at Brooklands in May of 1928. It was a handicap race with the team finishing in 3rd, 6th, and 8th places; Birkin, who was third, won the prize for the greatest distance covered.

At Le Mans in 1928 the team battled with a strong American contingent of Stutzes and Chryslers. Birkin lost three hours when he went off the road and Clement's car overheated. Sensationally, victory went to the 1927 survivor, driven by Barnato and Bernard Rubin. After a lapse of six years the Tourist Trophy was run as a sports car handicap on the Ards circuit outside Belfast in Northern Ireland, but the handicap was too stiff for the Bentleys and a fifth place by Birkin was the best that could be achieved.

It was impossible to hold a proper 24-hour race at Brooklands because racing at night was forbidden, but in 1929 the next best thing was arranged, a two-day race where cars ran for 12 hours each day and were impounded overnight. Known as the 'Double-Twelve', the race was run on a handicap basis and had 52 starters. It saw the debut of a new racing Bentley, the 6½-litre Speed Six which was driven by Barnato and Benjafield. It led the race for the first eight hours until the dynamo disintegrated. Sammy Davis, sharing a 4½ with Sir Roland Gunter, then took up the challenge and for the rest of the first day and all the second day, battled with a 1750 Alfa

Le Mans 1928. The winning 4½ litre of Woolf Barnato and Bernard Rubin leads a Stutz. This car was involved in the multi-car crash during the 1927 Race.

The first Bentley entry. John Duff lies under the car plugging a leaking fuel tank.

Le Mans 1924. The victorious 3.0 litre of Duff and Clement.

Tim Birkin in his 'Blower' Bentley at Brooklands in 1932.

SIR HENRY BIRKIN

Sir Henry Birkin, baronet, otherwise known as Tim, was the epitome of the glamorous 'Bentley Boy'. Like Segrave an RFC pilot in World War One, he made a tentative start by racing at Brooklands in 1921. He came into the sport properly in 1927, driving a Bentley, and was included in the Bentley works team in 1928. His reputation for fast, tough driving qualified him as the team's pacemaker. His first major win was in the Le Mans 24-Hours in 1929.

That year Tim Birkin began an association with the rich, racehorse-owning, Hon. Dorothy Paget. She sponsored his team of supercharged Bentleys, the 'Blower' cars, which was run separately from the works team. In one of the 'Blower' cars, a single-seater, Birkin became the hero of the Brooklands crowd, breaking the lap record twice and leaving it at 137.96 mph in 1932. Probably his greatest drive was in the 1930 French G.P. at Pau where he came second and almost won in a sports-bodied 'Blower'.

Paget's support diminished after 1930 and so Birkin drove Alfa Romeos and Maseratis. With an Alfa he won at Le Mans in 1931. He contracted malaria while driving a Maserati in the 1933 Tripoli G.P. and died soon afterwards. He was 37. His autobiography 'Full Throttle' was highly controversial for its savage attack on Brooklands and the management of British motor racing.

Romeo on handicap. At the end the Alfa was the winner by the narrow margin of 0.003 on the handicap formula.

The Speed Six redeemed itself at Le Mans. Driven by Barnato and Birkin it led home a Bentley 1-2-3-4, emphasised when the four Bentleys swept across the line in team order. The Speed Six did its stuff again by winning the Essex Six-Hour race at Brooklands, a fortnight after Le Mans. The Six-Hour race was the debut for a new Bentley, the supercharged 4½ litre, always known as the 'Blower Bentley'.

The 'Blower' was a private venture of driver Tim Birkin, built at his own works at Welwyn Garden City. While Birkin received encouragement from Barnato, the project did not have the approval of WO. The building of a team of 'Blowers' for racing was funded by the Hon. Dorothy Paget, a very rich heiress whose main passion was racehorses.

The 1929 season ended with the 500-mile race at Brooklands, organised by the British Racing Drivers Club, a club which had been virtually founded by the 'Bentley Boys'. This flat-out race around the banked bowl was won by an unblown 4½ driven by Clement and Jack Barclay at a speed of 107.32 mph while the Speed Six came second. The winning speed at Indianapolis that same year over the same distance was 97.59 mph.

Although all seemed set fair for Bentley, the financial storm clouds were gathering. Barnato and Clement won

Le Mans 1930. The Speed Sixes which dominated the race lead away at the start.

Eddie Hall in his 3½/4¼-litre Bentley which took second place in the Ulster Tourist Tophy in 1934, 1935 and 1936. The car went on to finish eighth at Le Mans in 1950.

were bought by Rolls-Royce. A 3½-litre Rolls-Royce-built Bentley was produced. Racing this six-cylinder car seemed most unlikely, but a 3½ with full Rolls-Royce support ran in the 1934 and 1935 Tourist Trophy, driven by Eddie Hall. With the later 4¼-litre engine it ran in the 1936 race. This unlikely racer proved its pedigree by finishing in second place in all three contests.

When the Le Mans 24-hour race was revived in 1949, a 4¼, which had been a 1939 factory prototype, appeared with a special aerodynamic saloon body and finished in a most creditable sixth place. It came back again in 1950 and came 14th. Hall joined in too with his TT car and finished 8th. That seemed to be the end of Bentley as a serious motor racing name although the cars continued to delight both owners and spectators in vintage and historic racing. In 1992 Stanley Mann, a noted Bentley restorer, broke British national class records up to 1,000 miles with the Bentley Jackson, a single-seater which had evolved from the 1928 Le Mans winner.

In 1980 Rolls-Royce had sold off its car division, which included Bentley, to Vickers. In 1998 Vickers agreed a deal with Volkswagen and BMW which put Bentley into VW's expanding portfolio. Audi, the high-performance division of VW, were running an extensive sports-car-racing programme. Based on their technology, in 2001 it was decided to revive the Bentley name in racing. The Bentley EXP Speed 8 was built in England by the specialist firm, Racing Technology Norfolk, using a turbocharged Audi 3.6-litre V-8 engine.

Two EXP Speed 8s ran at Le Mans in 2001 and one finished third behind two Audis. With an enlarged 4.0-litre engine, one car went to Le Mans in 2002 and came fourth behind an Audi trio. Then in 2003 two cars, now simply known as Speed 8s, had a preliminary canter in the Sebring 12-hour race before going to Le Mans. The outcome would have delighted WO as the green-painted cars came first and second, the winning car driven by Tom Kristensen, Guy Smith and Rinaldo Capello.

Although Audi's racing capabilities had helped put Bentley back on the map as a sporting marque, after the Le Mans win the venture was closed. Nevertheless Bentley continues to be run by men who prize very high performance, as their modern production cars demonstrate. Surely international motor racing has not seen the last of the powerful green Bentleys.

the 1930 Double-Twelve in a Speed Six and another Speed Six driven by Sammy Davis and Clive Dunfee was second. Then the team went to Le Mans where there was a titanic battle between Birkin's 'Blower' cars, running as a separate team, and the Mercedes-Benz of Rudolf Caracciola. The battle destroyed the contenders and left the Speed Sixes to take first and second. Barnato and Glen Kidston drove the winning car while Clement and Watney were second.

Immediately after Le Mans Bentley announced that it was withdrawing from racing. Barnato had decided he had had enough. With the start of the Great Depression, even his huge resources were feeling the pinch. Only Birkin soldiered on with his team of Paget-financed 'Blowers'.

Since the withdrawal of Sunbeam there had been no British participation in Grand Prix racing, but in September 1930 the daring Birkin took a stripped sports 'Blower' to the French G.P. at Pau and astounded the racing world by taking second place among the pure racing cars. Birkin raced his famous single-seater 'Blower' at Brooklands from 1930 to 1932, when it was the fastest car on the track, taking the lap record several times, its best being 137.96 mph.

In 1931 the Depression forced Bentley Motors into liquidation. After both negotiation and litigation, the assets

The Bentley Speed 8, built in England and powered by a turbocharged Audi 4.0-litre V-8 engine. It is seen here on its way to victory at Le Mans in 2003. Another Speed 8 came in second.

CHAPTER 5

MG: Racing Cars for Everyman

THE seeds of MG were sown in 1921 when Cecil Kimber joined Morris Garages, a retail outlet of Morris Motors – on the brink of becoming a major manufacturer – centred in Oxford. Kimber began fitting sporting bodies to modified and tuned Morris Cowleys and Oxfords. From 1926 these were marketed as 'MG' cars.

In 1927 Morris bought the Wolseley company, which had in its dowry the design for a small overhead-camshaft engine. This engine went into the Morris Minor, which Kimber reworked with a neat, two-seat sports body. With mild engine tuning it became the M-type MG, built in a dedicated MG factory at Abingdon, near Oxford.

The M-type was immediately accepted by sporting owners. One of the first was the Earl of March, who after World War Two, as the Duke of Richmond and Gordon, established the Goodwood racing circuit. March raced an M-type in minor meetings at Brooklands in 1929. In 1930 a team of M-types took the team prize in the Double-Twelve race at the track.

The closest rival of MG in the small sports car market was Austin. There was rivalry between the two companies to achieve the honour of being the first to exceed 100 mph with a 750 cc car. A special single-seat MG using many M-type parts exceeded the 100 mph target at Montlhéry

in February 1931, driven by George Eyston. From this a new sports-racing MG, the 750 cc C-type, was developed in a few months by Hubert Charles, the chief designer.

The horde of C-types entered for the 1931 Double-Twelve dominated the race on handicap, taking the first five places, the winning car driven by March and Chris Staniland. This was the start of a marvellous year for MG and the C-type. Norman Black won the Irish Grand Prix in Phoenix Park, Dublin, and went on to win the Ulster Tourist Trophy where another MG was third. To get the best advantage of the handicaps given the cars in the TT, superchargers were fitted. From then on until 1935, with few exceptions, all racing MGs were supercharged.

The 1932 season was less successful for MG because in the major British sports car races, which were run as handicaps, the handicappers were no longer in the dark about the C-type's performance. The Ulster driver, Hugh Hamilton, scored the first international success for MG in winning the 750 cc class of the German Grand Prix at the Nürburgring. At the end of 1932 a C-type with a single-seat body won the BRDC 500-mile race at Brooklands driven by Birmingham brewery heir Ron Horton. A special record-breaker, EX 120, had been built. George Eyston took this and a new production J3 to

CECIL KIMBER

Cecil Kimber was the guiding force who established MG as the first mass producer of sports cars. Born in 1888, he worked for the luxury-car manufacturer Sheffield Simplex before World War One. After Kimber's spell at AC, William Morris (later Lord Nuffield) appointed him as manager of Morris Garages, the Oxford retail outlet of the burgeoning Morris Motors. Seeing a profitable opportunity, Kimber began making sports versions of the Morris which soon grew into the MG, built in a separate factory at Abingdon.

A salesman, not an engineer, Kimber knew what the market wanted. He encouraged his designer, Hubert Charles, to develop a wide range of MG sports cars which were produced in their thousands to satisfy an eager public. The early MGs were soon raced and in a few short years were developed into formidable competition cars capable of winning anything from major races to mud trials.

Nuffield, who owned MG personally, sold the company to his Nuffield Group in 1935. It was a difficult time for Kimber, whose audacious policies and methods were at variance with Nuffield's conservative directors and accountants. He left MG during World War Two, then worked for the Specialloid Piston company. Kimber was killed in a railway accident in 1945.

Montlhéry in December 1932. EX 120 achieved 120 mph and between them the partnership took every 750 cc class record up to 24 hours.

It was MG's policy that its racing cars had to be based on production parts, of which many were interchangeable with their standard components. Wolseley had produced a six-cylinder 1,271 cc engine for its Hornet. MG used this for its sports-touring F-type Magna, but it was unsuitable for development as a racing engine and so a new engine was designed which was effectively a C-type with six cylinders. This went into the touring and sports MG Magnette.

During the winter of 1932/33 a racing version was developed which became the legendary blown 1,086 cc

Lord March in his C-type MG during his winning drive in the 1931 Double-12 at Brooklands. Subsequently, as the Duke of Richmond he founded the Goodwood circuit.

Tazio Nuvolari winning the 1933 Ulster Tourist Trophy in a K3 MG.

K3 MG. The K3 made its racing debut in the 1933 Mille Miglia, the 1,000-mile race run on open roads in Italy, starting in Brescia and returning there via Rome and Florence. In a superb result, a team of three cars won the 1,100 cc class and the team prize.

There were some teething problems during the first part of the 1933 season, but in August the Anglo-American millionaire, Whitney Straight, took a K3 to Pescara in Italy and won the Coppa Acerbo *voiturette* race. This greatly discomfited the Italians and the French, who regarded the small racing classes as their eminent domain. A protest was lodged that the K3 had an oversized engine but when stripped it was found to be wholly legal. The Continentals had to grant that serious opposition was coming from Britain.

Of the several K3s entered for the Ulster Tourist Trophy in September one was offered to Tazio Nuvolari, then probably the premier driver in Grand Prix racing. Nuvolari took up the offer, being paid a fee of £100 by Sir William Morris (later Lord Nuffield) and in an electrifying and heroic drive, winning the handicap race. It was close, since Hugh Hamilton in a 750 cc J4 MG would have won but for a bungled pit stop. Earlier in the season Hamilton had won the 800 cc class in the Eifelrennen at the Nürburgring in his supercharged J4.

To show enthusiasts that less exotic MGs were potent cars too, a team of 1,086 cc L2 Magnas had been entered in the 200-mile LCC Relay Race at Brooklands in July. They won, with the same cars going on to win the team prize in the gruelling Alpine Trial, spending a week rushing up and down mountain passes. The season ended with the BRDC 500-mile race at Brooklands in which a K3 driven by Eddie Hall was the winner. The hard-used team of L2s came out again with one of these coming second, driven by Charles Martin and averaging 92.24 mph, an impressive speed for an almost standard car.

The roadgoing Magnas and J2 Midgets were making their mark as well, providing a relatively inexpensive means of letting enthusiasts enjoy all types of motor sport. MGs scored several wins at the new road circuit which opened at Donington Park at the beginning of 1933.

Improved for 1934, the K3 was joined by the Q-type, a new 750 cc car, while the P-type Midget and the N-type Magnette had replaced the J-type and L-type road cars. K3s took the first five places in the Mannin Beg, a 1,500 cc race run around the streets of Douglas in the Isle of Man. Then George Eyston won the British Empire Trophy at Brooklands in EX 135, a special semi-single-seat K3.

The success of the K3 on the Continent continued. Hamilton won the Coppa Acerbo at Pescara and the Italian, Rafaele Cecchini, was second in another K3. He had been so impressed with Straight's performance in 1933 that he had bought a K3, becoming the 1934 Italian 1,100 cc champion. Third at Pescara was a newcomer, Richard Seaman, driving Straight's car. A week later Seaman scored his first major win at Bern, coming first with the K3 in the Prix de Berne which preceded the Swiss Grand Prix. This started Seaman on the path which ultimately led him to become a member of the Mercedes-Benz Grand Prix team. Sadly Hugh Hamilton, who had done so much for MG, crashed fatally while driving a Maserati in the Swiss Grand Prix.

Kenneth Evans in a C-type MG at an early Donington Park meeting.

Bobbie Baird in the advanced R-type MG during the 1935 Mannin Beg in the Isle of Man.

The regulations for the 1934 Tourist Trophy banned supercharged cars, but the enthusiastic and resourceful competition department at Abingdon responded with a new car, the NE-type Magnette, virtually a standard N-type with a racing body and some mild tuning. Their 1,286 cc engine capacity gave the NEs a better handicap than the full 1,500 cc cars. Six were entered. The cars were quick, one coming home the winner, driven by Charlie Dodson. Dodson scored a rare double, as he had previously been a winner of the motorcycle TT in the Isle of Man.

During the winter of 1934-35 Hubert Charles designed a revolutionary racing car, the R-type. Apart from record-breakers, this was the first and only MG designed from scratch as a single-seater. With its torsion-bar independent suspension on all four wheels and a backbone chassis frame it was at the forefront of international design and greatly in advance of any other British machine. Fitted initially with the Q-type's 750 cc engine, the R-type was planned to be uprated to a

1,500 cc engine during development, giving it the potential to compete as a *voiturette*.

The R-type appeared in the early races of the 1935 season and showed that it needed development. In the same year a team of 939 cc sports PBs was entered for the Le Mans 24-hour race. Driven by a team of lady drivers, cheekily dubbed 'George Eyston's dancing daughters' by the press after their team manager, the three cars finished and made a most favourable impression.

MG had been owned personally by Lord Nuffield, as Sir William Morris had become. At the beginning of 1935 he sold MG to the newly formed Nuffield Group. Leonard Lord, the group's new chairman, decided that racing was too costly and in July 1935 the Abingdon racing department was closed and all racing activity ceased. MG racing was left in the hands of private owners.

Gradually, in the years running up to World War Two, the cars made less impact as newer and quicker machines appeared. MG was still prominent in the record-breaking world. A special 750 cc car, the 'Magic

Goldie Gardner's team wait with MG EX 135 at Dessau, Germany, in 1939 before his record-breaking runs. The Nazi stormtroopers seem unimpressed.

Midget', had been built for George Eyston and was the first 750 to exceed 120 mph. This was sold to a German, Robert Kohlrausch, who pushed the record to over 140 mph in 1936. Mercedes-Benz was so impressed by its engine's 164 bhp output that it acquired it for investigation.

Lt. Col. Goldie Gardner, who had been an active MG racer, had broken several 1,100 cc class records with a K3. He now bought EX 135, a special single-seater K3 that had been built for George Eyston. Extensively tuned and modified by the Abingdon team, it was fitted with an all-enveloping body designed by Reid Railton, whom we met earlier as designer of Napier-powered cars for John Cobb.

Early in 1939 the beautifully low and sleek EX 135 was taken to Germany. On a special section of autobahn at Dessau, Gardner achieved 203 mph to take the 1,100 cc class mile and kilometre records. The car was then stripped in a local garage and bored out just enough to put it into the 1,500 cc class. A few days later it took the 1,500 cc world record at 204 mph.

After World War Two, Gardner brought EX 135 out again. With its engine reduced to 750 cc he took the class mile and kilometre records at over 150 mph on the Jabbeke motorway in Belgium. With an experimental 2.0-litre four-cylinder XK Jaguar engine fitted, the 2,000 cc class record also fell at 177 mph.

Gardner and his team of Abingdon experts had not finished. Running the six-cylinder engine on three cylinders to give a 500 cc capacity, EX 135 took that class record at over 150 mph. Finally in July 1950, with the venerable K3 engine running with two cylinders, the

The MGA team at Le Mans in 1955.

George Eyston and Syd Enever, the MG development engineer, with the 1957 MG record-breaker EX 181.

350 cc class record fell at 120 mph. When EX 135 retired it was the fastest car in international classes from 350 cc to 2,000 cc.

In 1957 a new teardrop-shaped record car, EX 181, was built with a blown twin-cam MGA engine in the rear. With this, Stirling Moss raised the 1,500 cc flying kilometre record to 245.64 mph at Bonneville, Utah. In 1958 Phil Hill raised this record again with EX 181 to 254.91 mph. 'Roaring Raindrop' was this sleek car's appropriate nickname.

In the early post-war years MG competition activity was restricted to private entries in rallies and production-car racing. In 1954, however, the British Motor Corporation – of which MG had become a part – reopened the competition department at Abingdon for an intensive racing and rallying programme using production cars. Its first venture was a team of the new MGA sports cars at Le Mans and in the Tourist Trophy in 1955.

The MGAs and subsequent MGBs, painted in the BMC colour scheme of red and white, appeared not only in rallies but also in the classic long-distance races where class wins were gained. A notable outright win was scored at the Nürburgring in 1966 when an MGB driven by Julien Vernaeve and Andrew Hedges won the Marathon de la Route, an 84-hour race *cum* regularity event.

These heady years ended in 1969, when British Leyland, as BMC had become, closed the competition department and the Abingdon factory was sold. British Leyland subsequently became the Rover Group which was nationalised and sold to British Aerospace in 1988; BAe sold the car business to BMW in 1994. The Germans passed it on to the Phoenix Consortium in 2000 when it became MG Rover. The MG name passed into Chinese hands when the Consortium sold its interests.

In 2001 the owners of MG Rover returned to motor racing with the MG-Lola EX 257, using a turbocharged 2.0-litre four-cylinder engine, based on production parts, in a sports-racing Lola chassis. The car was entered for the Le Mans Prototype 675 class. No success came in 2001 but in 2002 a car won the LMP 675 class at Sebring and continued to dominate the class in USA racing for the rest of the season.

In 2003 a Judd V-8 KV 675 engine replaced the MG unit but without the much-desired success at Le Mans. At the end of the season the MG Rover Group cancelled the project. Now merely bearing the MG name, the cars continued to be developed and raced in Europe by Britain's Ray Mallock Ltd and by the Dyson team in the USA with some success up to 2007. The prospect can not be excluded that the MG's new Chinese owners will see merit in drawing on the marque's great sporting heritage.

An MGB in the pits during the 1966 1000 kms at the Nurburgring. A similar car won the 1966 72-hour Marathon de la Route on the same circuit.

CHAPTER 6

ERA: Enduring Racing Automobile

R AYMOND MAYS was the leading British hill climb competitor in the 1920s, driving Bugattis, ACs and the Vauxhall Villiers, a car developed from a 1922 TT Vauxhall. Mays ran the Vauxhall Villiers until 1933, but then needed a new car to break the course record at the Shelsley Walsh hill climb, a venue with which he had strong associations.

The persuasive Mays approached the Riley Motor Company, who agreed to loan him a 1932-33 1,500 cc racing Riley 12/6 chassis and engine. The six-cylinder Riley engine was extensively modified, partially redesigned and supercharged. The design was by Murray Jamieson who had already produced impressive results with the works racing Austin Sevens. He was aided by Peter Berthon, an ex-RAF officer who was a close friend of Mays.

The completed car, painted white and hence known as 'The White Riley', achieved Mays's aim and broke the Shelsley record in June 1933. It went on to take the class lap record on the Mountain circuit at Brooklands. Noting the Riley's pace, Humphrey Cook approached Mays. Cook, who had been racing since 1914 and had sold the 1922 TT Vauxhall to Mays, was concerned that British prestige was low in international racing. He believed that

the Riley could be developed into a successful car to compete in international *voiturette* races for cars up to 1,500 cc, a class of racing which had become very active in Europe. The wealthy Cook was both able and willing to back the construction and racing of a team of cars which would also be manufactured for sale.

English Racing Automobiles Ltd (ERA) was formed in November 1933, funded by Cook, with Cook, Mays and Berthon as directors. A workshop was built in the grounds of the Mays' house at Bourne in Lincolnshire. Jamieson continued his development of the engine, producing what had become a new design, while Reid Railton was engaged to design a conventional single-seat chassis around the engine, using a preselector gearbox. Railton, who had worked with Parry Thomas, had designed later developments of Campbell's 'Blue Bird' and been responsible for the chassis of the very successful Brooklands Riley sports car.

Painted a pale apple green, the first ERA was finished in the spring of 1934. It was entered for the Mannin Beg, a 1,500 cc race in the streets of Douglas, Isle of Man, but did not start as there were handling problems. The car then ran in the 300-mile British Empire Trophy at Brooklands driven by Mays and Cook and finished, although it was delayed by minor bothers.

A second car with an 1,100 cc engine scored ERA's first victory at the 1934 Brooklands August Bank Holiday meeting, driven appropriately by Cook. A third car with a 2.0-litre engine made best time of the day at Shelsley. Then Mays capped ERA's debut season by taking the World Standing Start kilometre record at Brooklands with the 2.0-litre car. He also won the 100-mile Nuffield Trophy at Donington Park with the 1,500 cc car.

The successes brought orders from several drivers for the 1935 season. With the ERA offered for sale at £1,700, the first customer was Pat Fairfield, a South African living in England, while the second buyer was Richard Seaman, an intensely ambitious driver who saw the ERA as a stepping stone in his aim to become a full Grand Prix driver. The first three cars and that of Fairfield were the A-types and Seaman had the first B-type. The main

Raymond Mays in 'The White Riley' at Brooklands in 1933. Murray Jamieson, who was responsible for much of the engine design, stands on the right and Peter Berthon pushes on the cockpit edge.

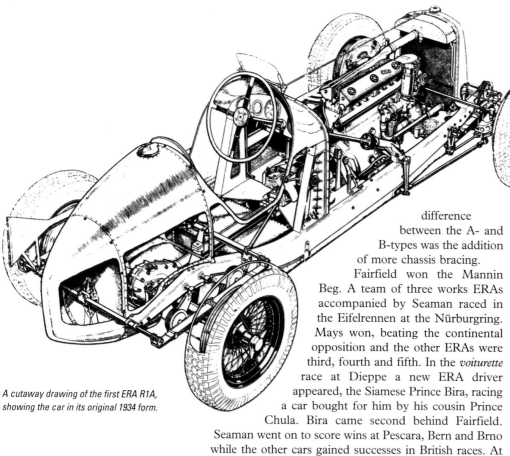

A cutaway drawing of the first ERA R1A, showing the car in its original 1934 form.

difference between the A- and B-types was the addition of more chassis bracing.

Fairfield won the Mannin Beg. A team of three works ERAs accompanied by Seaman raced in the Eifelrennen at the Nürburgring. Mays won, beating the continental opposition and the other ERAs were third, fourth and fifth. In the *voiturette* race at Dieppe a new ERA driver appeared, the Siamese Prince Bira, racing a car bought for him by his cousin Prince Chula. Bira came second behind Fairfield. Seaman went on to score wins at Pescara, Bern and Brno while the other cars gained successes in British races. At the end of the 1935 season, Cook's ambition had been achieved. The ERA was the car to beat in the *voiturette* class.

The 1936 season was a setback for the ERA team. Trying to cope with the needs of both customers and the works, the cars were poorly prepared. Attempts to gain a big power increase using a Zoller supercharger were offset by unreliability. Some nine B-types had gone to customers, but Bira was the most successful driver. His main opposition came from Seaman, who had abandoned his ERA for a rebuilt 1927 GP Delage which was more than a match for the ERAs. Bira won at Monaco and Albi and other owners won lesser events in England and Ireland.

During the winter of 1936-37 two works B-types were fitted with Porsche-type trailing-arm independent front suspension and the now-reliable Zoller blower, and became known as C-types. In addition to Bira in his B-type, the black-painted C-types, driven by Mays and Fairfield – and by Arthur Dobson after Fairfield was killed

in a crash in the Le Mans 24-hour race – were unbeatable in European *voiturette* races and also dominated British events. Charles Martin in an A-type won a remarkable race on Berlin's Avus track with its two fast straights and banked turn.

While the ERAs were still on top in British races in 1938, they began to struggle in European *voiturette* races. The German dominance in Grands Prix forced Alfa Romeo and Maserati to concentrate on the 1,500 cc class. Both produced new cars, of which the Type 158 Alfa was to become one of the all-time great racing designs, so the now-ageing ERAs had little success in the international *voiturette* class. Wins for Bira at Cork and Mays at Peronne were all that could be achieved away from home.

Modified and updated at the beginning of 1938, Raymond Mays's C-type had become the D-type. The Grand Prix formula had been changed at the end of 1937 with a sliding scale of weights and capacity limits up to 3.0 litres for supercharged cars and 4½ litres for unsupercharged cars. Mays and Berthon decided they would build a full Grand Prix car, aiming at a light 2½ litre machine, but their ambitions vastly outran Cook's diminishing resources.

Murray Jamieson had been killed when a car ran into the crowd at a Brooklands race early in 1938 – a great loss to British racing car engineering – so Berthon and Arthur Barratt designed the new E-type ERA. It was realised towards the end of 1938 that a full GP car was not feasible and so the design became a new 1,500 cc *voiturette,* with the long-term aim of it becoming a GP car with the formula expected to change to a 1,500 cc supercharged limit in 1940.

At the beginning of 1939 relations among Cook, Mays and Berthon became strained to breaking point. Cook felt unable to put any more money into the venture. Mays and Berthon departed, taking the D-type – known as the legendary R4D – while Cook, deciding to carry on as the newly formed British Motor Racing Fund, tried to find support for the new E-type. The new ERA was finished in the spring of 1939, but although seemingly an advanced design and clearly a beautiful looking car, it was a disaster. The detail work of the design had considerable shortcomings and the workmanship was not up to the task.

The new car was fast. At Albi, in its only race in 1939, it led until it broke down. For the B- and C-types the days of dominance were over. The 158 Alfa was in a different class; the 4CL Maserati had the advantages of a later design and the W165 Mercedes-Benz, which made an astonishing victorious debut at Tripoli in 1939, made the E-type look a hopeless venture.

When motor racing resumed after World War Two it was a very different sport. The German teams which had dominated Grand Prix racing had gone. In 1946 the first racing was sketchy, supported primarily by amateur teams. The only professional team was state-owned Alfa Romeo, which had been kept intact during the conflict and had emerged even stronger than before.

There was no circuit racing in England because both Brooklands and Donington had been lost, while racing on road circuits, so popular on the continent, was prohibited. Many of the ERAs were in the hands of new drivers who had nowhere to race except sprints and hill climbs.

The first major post-war race was the G.P. des Nations at Geneva in July 1946, run for 1,500 cc cars. This set the pattern for the next five years as it was dominated by the Tipo 158 Alfas. Several ERAs took part, the best result a sixth place by Bira. Humphrey Cook had kept ERA Ltd going in a factory moved to Dunstable, north of London. The first E-type was sold to Peter Whitehead who took it to the Turin G.P. where it failed. A second car, already under construction in 1939, was completed. ERA announced that a batch of six E-types would be built and offered for sale at £5,000, a heady notion which did not in fact eventuate.

In 1947 a new Grand Prix formula was introduced for 1½-litre supercharged and 4½-litre unsupercharged cars, so many ERAs were now full Grand Prix cars. The elevated status made little difference as the racing in 1947 was dominated by the 158 Alfa, but those drivers who took ERAs to continental G.Ps were able to pick up places by reliability. Among the new owners was Bob Gerard who had bought an A-type and a B-type. With the latter he showed that good preparation and steady driving paid dividends, coming fourth in the G.P. d'Europe at Spa and third at Reims; at home, he won the Ulster Trophy and the British Empire Trophy in the Isle of Man.

The first E-type, now owned by Reg Parnell, continued to disappoint. To gain reliability both cars were de-tuned, so were slower than the best B-types. At the end of 1947 Cook sold ERA Ltd to the entrepreneurial Leslie Johnson, who was one of the post-war generation of drivers. Stating his intention of persevering with the E-type, Johnson bought the second car back from its unhappy owner.

Gerard continued with his success in 1948, winning the Jersey Road Race in the Channel Islands. Circuit racing resumed in England toward the end of 1948 with the opening of tracks on former airfields at Goodwood

DICK SEAMAN

At a time when most British racing drivers revelled in their amateur approach to the sport, Dick Seaman had a tough, professional attitude which took him to the top. After driving a Bugatti in minor British races, he became noticed when he bought a K3 MG in 1934. With the K3 he won the Prix de Berne, regarded then as the principal European *voiturette* race.

For 1935 Seaman bought a new ERA which was maintained by its makers. After a frustrating start to the season with mechanical failures, he set up his own organisation to prepare the ERA. He then swept the board and was unbeatable in European 1.5-litre races. In 1936, aided by the gifted mechanic, Giulio Ramponi, Seaman raced a modified 1927 GP Delage and was the acknowledged king of the *voiturette* class.

Mercedes-Benz spotted Seaman's talent and signed him as a member of their Grand Prix team in 1937. He picked up several places but his great win came in 1938 when he was victorious in the German G.P. Never one to avoid risk at the wheel, Dick Seaman was killed after his Mercedes slid off the wet course in the 1939 Belgian G.P. while in the lead.

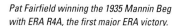

Pat Fairfield winning the 1935 Mannin Beg with ERA R4A, the first major ERA victory.

and Silverstone. In the British G.P. at Silverstone, Gerard was third behind the Maseratis of Gigi Villoresi and Alberto Ascari. Although preoccupied with the birth pains of the BRM project, Mays raced R4D occasionally, gaining some places, but primarily concentrated on hill climbs and won the newly instituted RAC Hill Climb Championship in 1947 and 1948.

In 1949 the pattern was much the same. Alfa Romeo had withdrawn from G.P. racing for a year but there was a new force, Ferrari. Continental organisers were becoming reluctant to accept ERA entries, feeling the cars looked out-of-date and were becoming even less competitive. Only Gerard and Cuth Harrison, who had a C-type with modernised bodywork, were capable of keeping up with the pace of the mid-field.

A new era began in 1950 with the creation of the F1 World Championship. In the very first event at Silverstone both E-types fell out, but Gerard and Harrison were sixth and seventh, a long way behind the victorious Alfa

Romeos. At Monza in September there was the last sad appearance of an ERA in a Continental F1 event when Harrison retired with his C-type.

Although outpaced in post-war G.P. racing, the ERAs and their plucky owners had waved the British flag valiantly. Without their efforts there would have been no British participation at the top level of the sport in the immediate post-war years. Since 1951 the cars have continued to delight the crowds at vintage and historic events. They are racing as strongly as ever and will do so for many years to come.

There was a tantalising postscript. At the end of 1951 Alfa Romeo withdrew from Grand Prix racing. With the mainstay gone, in 1952 races in the subsidiary Formula 2 for unsupercharged 2.0-litre cars became the events that qualified for the World Championship for Drivers. Leslie Johnson had long since abandoned the E-type and engaged David Hodkin to design a car to suit Formula 2.

1935 ERA B-Type

Many of the successes gained by ERA between 1934 and 1939 were scored by the Siamese Prince Bira, driving cars owned by his cousin, Prince Chula, whose White Mouse Stable team was based in London. His favourite car was the B-type ERA 'Romulus' with which Bira had his first win in the 1,500 cc supporting race at Monaco in 1936. It was painted in the distinctive colour which became known as 'Bira blue.'

Johnnie Wakefield on the start line of the 1939 British Empire Trophy. His car R14B was the last B/C type to be built.

The new ERA was the G-type, which had a highly tuned Bristol six-cylinder engine in a very light and rigid ladder-type chassis made of huge magnesium tubes. It was unusual in having an offset driving position that suited it as the basis of a possible sports car. Up-and-coming Stirling Moss was engaged as the driver, but like the E-type it was unreliable on its few outings and finished only once in a minor race.

At the end of 1952 Johnson sold the whole project to Bristol, which had turned to making cars after the war. Bristol developed this into its Type 450 sports-racing model, which in both coupé and open forms scored many 2.0 litre class wins, including Le Mans in 1954 and 1955. Although ERA Ltd faded away from the sport, becoming an engineering research company, the initials ERA had achieved immortality.

Raymond Mays in ERA R4D at the 1946 G.P. des Nations, the first major post-war race.

Bob Gerard with ERA R14B in the 1950 British Grand Prix, the first race ever held for the World Championship.

Peter Whitehead tests the E-type ERA in 1946.

Stirling Moss in the G-type ERA during the 1952 British Grand Prix.

CHAPTER 7

Aston Martin: The Long Quest for Glory

IN 1914 Robert Bamford and Lionel Martin, trading as Bamford & Martin Ltd, were tuning 10 hp Singers for competition. At their small works in West Kensington, London they built a car with an Isotta-Fraschini chassis and Coventry Simplex engine which was called an Aston Martin, the 'Aston' coming from the Aston Clinton hill climb where Martin had been successful.

World War One intervened but in 1920 the first true Aston Martin appeared with a 1,500 cc side-valve engine in a conventional chassis. Martin used this extensively in competition and raced it at Brooklands in 1920. Bamford had left the company, but in 1921 the legendary Count Louis Zborowski, better known for his 'Chitty, Bang, Bang' cars, introduced new capital. Four cars ran in the 1921 JCC 200-Mile race at Brooklands and Zborowski's had an overhead-cam engine.

Next year Zborowski financed two new cars which had twin-overhead-cam engines. These ran in the French G.P. at Strasbourg, though handicapped by their 1.5-litre engines while the rest of the field were of 2.0-litre capacity. In September 1922 Zborowski came second in a GP car in the Gran Premio do Penya Rhin in Spain. At Brooklands, the GP cars failed in the 200-Mile race, but G.C. Stead in a side-valve Aston Martin took second place, splitting the powerful Talbot-Darracq team.

Earlier in 1922 a side-valve car broke ten World long-distance records and many 1,500 cc class records at Brooklands, becoming the first car under 1.5-litres to hold World records. In 1923 Zborowski again took second place at Penya Rhin, but then the first of recurring financial crises beset Aston Martin, partly exacerbated by Zborowski's death in a Mercedes at Monza in 1924. Control of the company passed to the Charnwood family, but the money problems continued and a receiver was appointed in 1926.

Italian by birth, Augustus Bertelli, always known as 'Bert', had been developing the Enfield Allday sports car for a company in Birmingham. When that project was wound up, Bertelli joined forces with engineer William Renwick. They built the R&B car, funded by Renwick who had inherited a fortune. Renwick designed a sturdy single-overhead-cam four for the R&B. In the midst of this, the pair were approached by the Hon. John Benson of the Charnwood family. It was agreed that Bertelli and Renwick would buy the remains of the old Aston Martin company.

A factory was found at Feltham, near the present Heathrow Airport, and a new car, using a development of Renwick's engine, with a low sporting chassis, was announced at the end of 1927. With the new firm in dire financial straits Benson and Renwick pulled out, but Bertelli found more backers and the car, the International, went into production.

Racing was immediately on Aston Martin's agenda. A team ran at Le Mans in 1928 and took part in the long-distance sports car races at Brooklands, gaining a class win in the 1930 Double-Twelve. Aston repeated this in 1931, followed by a class win in the Tourist Trophy. In trouble once more, the company was tided over by help from H.J. Aldington of Frazer Nash cars until Bertelli found long-term finance from Lance Prideaux-Brune, a London car dealer.

The first major competition success came in 1932 with a racing version of the new Le Mans model, driven by Bertelli and Pat Driscoll to win the Biennial Cup at Le Mans, an index of performance where a car had to qualify the previous year to compete for the Cup. A development of the Le Mans appeared in 1934 which was to evolve into the coveted Ulster model, in its sleek cycle-winged lines the *ne plus ultra* of small-displacement British competition cars.

Another Tourist Trophy class win in 1934 was followed by an excellent season in 1935. Aston Martin now had a reputation for being a tough, reliable long-distance racer. An Ulster won its class in the Mille Miglia. Then at Le Mans an outright third place was gained by Charles Martin and Charles Brackenbury in a works Ulster, also securing the Biennial Cup for the second time. These works cars forsook racing green for a bright red. Red was also relevant on the financial side, where Prideaux-Brune had not been able to keep up with expenditure. In 1933 Sir Arthur Sutherland, a shipping magnate, bought the company and installed his son Gordon as managing director.

Based on the existing engine Bertelli had developed a new 2.0-litre car which was raced from 1936 up to the outbreak of World War Two. Although quick it was up against the more advanced 328 BMW in its class.

The 1922 Grand Prix Aston Martin.

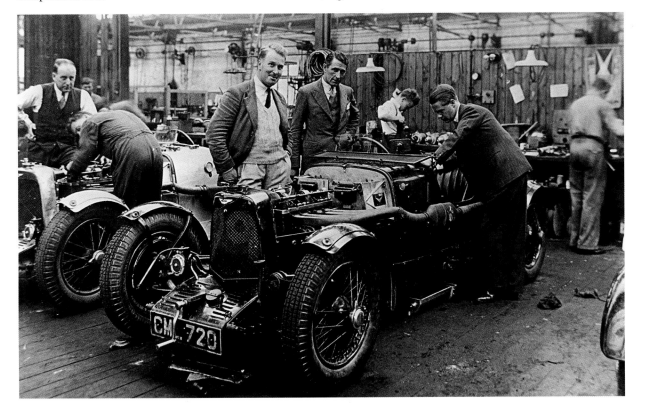

Charles Brackenbury and A.C. 'Bert' Bertelli stand behind the 1½-litre Aston Martin which won the Biennial Cup and the Index of Performance at Le Mans in 1935, while it is prepared in the Feltham factory for the Ulster Tourist Trophy.

The 2.0-litre Aston Martin which won the Biennial Cup at Le Mans in 1937 makes a pit stop during the 1938 race.

Jock Horsfall with the DB1 which won the 1948 Spa 24-hour race. Claude Hill, the designer, stands behind the car.

advanced space-frame saloon with a 2.0-litre four-cylinder pushrod engine. In 1947 the Sutherland family sold the company to the industrialist, David Brown. In 1948 a sports-racing development of the 'Atom', the DB1, won the Spa 24-hour race in Belgium driven by Leslie Johnson and Jock Horsfall. Le Mans had not yet resumed activity and so it was a most prestigious victory.

Under W.O. Bentley, who had joined Lagonda in the mid-1930s, Willie Watson had designed the post-war six-cylinder 2.6-litre Lagonda engine. Brown saw the possibilities of this twin-overhead-cam engine and to obtain it he bought Lagonda in 1948. Next year Le Mans was revived and a handsome new Aston Martin coupé appeared, fitted with the Lagonda engine, thus becoming the famous DB2. The DB2, which became a production model, was mildly tuned and raced extensively in 1950 and 1951, winning the Index of Performance at Le Mans in 1950.

In 1952 a proper sports-racing Aston Martin appeared, the DB3 with a 2.6-litre engine in a chassis designed by Eberan von Eberhorst, the former Auto Union designer. Though not notably successful, the DB3 managed a win in the 1952 Goodwood Nine Hours driven by Peter Collins and Pat Griffith. Redesigned for 1953, it became the 2.9-litre DB3S.

This much more attractive and successful car won the Nine Hours again with Reg Parnell and Eric Thompson and more importantly took first and second places in the Tourist Trophy at Dundrod in Northern Ireland, Collins and Griffith being the winners. The year 1954 was poor, but in 1955 the Nine Hours was won again, this time by Peter Walker and Dennis Poore. At the top level, Collins and Paul Frère took a DB3S into second place in the Le Mans 24-hour race, that year marred by the terrible Mercedes crash.

A new car, the DBR1, came out in 1956 and initially backed the now obsolescent DB3S. Designed by Ted Cutting, this had a 2,493 cc engine in a light space-frame chassis. Although a much larger car, it was considerably lighter than the DB3S. The DBR1 had a 3.0-litre engine for 1957 and gained results. Its big win was in the 1,000 kms at the Nürburgring where Tony Brooks and Noel Cunningham-Reid beat the cream of the opposition. Brooks went on to win the Belgian Sports Car G.P at Spa.

From 1958 the World Sports Championship was limited to 3.0-litre cars, but for lesser events a new chassis was built to carry 3.7- and later 3.9-litre engines, becoming the DBR2. The Nürburgring victory was repeated in 1958 with Stirling Moss and Jack Brabham as the drivers. Moss, paired with Brooks, led home an Aston

Nevertheless the Biennial Cup was won again in 1937 by a 2.0-litre driven by Mortimer Morris-Goodall and Robert Hichens. Hichens was to become a much decorated war hero in small naval craft before being killed in action in 1943.

Bertelli, who had an unhappy relationship with Sutherland, left the company in 1937. He was succeeded as designer by Claude Hill who produced the prototype 'Atom' just as World War Two began. This was an

Peter Collins (right) with Juan Manuel Fangio

PETER COLLINS

Peter Collins was one of the first of many talented drivers who emerged from the 500 cc racing class which grew so rapidly in the years just after World War Two. He began racing a Cooper in 1949 when he was 17. John Heath signed him up for his F2 HWM team in 1952.

He was also noticed by Aston Martin's renowned team manager, John Wyer.

With Aston Martin Collins won the 1952 Goodwood Nine Hours and the 1953 Tourist Trophy. Staying with Aston Martin for several seasons, he finished second at Le Mans in 1955 and 1956, driving a DB3S. Tony Vandervell engaged him both to drive the 4.5-litre Thin Wall Ferrari and to give the prototype Vanwall its first Grand Prix outing in 1954. For 1955 he was with BRM, racing the team's 250F Maserati until the Type 25 was ready.

Spotting the handsome Briton's talent, Enzo Ferrari signed Collins for 1956. He had a magnificent season, winning the French and Belgian G.Ps in the D50 Lancia-Ferrari. He had a sniff of the World Championship but in a sporting gesture handed his car over to team leader Juan Fangio in the Italian G.P., letting Fangio take the title and forfeiting his own chances.

In 1957 Collins was joined at Ferrari by his great friend and 'Mon Ami Mate' Mike Hawthorn, but it was a thin year. In 1958 he won the British G.P. in a Dino 246 Ferrari but a few weeks later was killed when he crashed in the German G.P. at the Nürburgring.

Roy Salvadori in a DB3S at Silverstone in 1956.

Roy Salvadori in a DBR1/300 Aston Martin at Le Mans in 1958. The car retired after 49 laps when it was damaged in an accident.

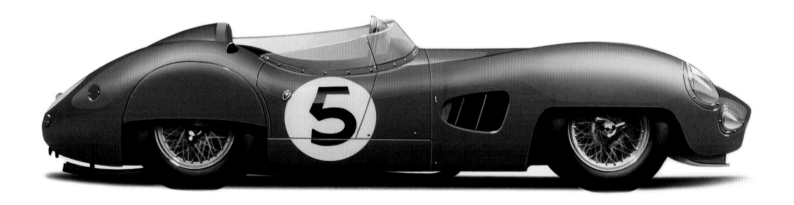

1959 Aston Martin DBR1

In 1959, the 3.0-litre DBR1 Aston Martin, driven by Roy Salvadori and Carroll Shelby won the Le Mans 24-hour race. With wins also in the Nürburgring 1,000 kms and in the Tourist Trophy at Goodwood, the DBR1 clinched the 1959 World Sports Car Championship for Aston Martin.

The unsuccessful DBR4 Grand Prix car at its Silverstone debut in 1959.

Aston Martin's withdrawal from sports car racing was short-lived. In the early 1960s a series of Grand Touring prototypes appeared: the DP212, DP214 and DP215, loosely derived from the current DB4 road car. These were the years when the 250 GTO Ferrari was at its apogee so results were sparse, though there was one notable success. Roy Salvadori took DP214 to Monza for the 1963 Inter-Europa Cup and beat the GTO Ferraris on their home ground.

In the late 1960s a new 5.0-litre four-camshaft V-8 engine was being developed for the Aston Martin road cars and a prototype was fitted to a Lola T70 GT. This ran at Le Mans in 1967 but lasted a mere seven laps, to the frustration of John Surtees who supported the project.

David Brown sold Aston Martin to Company Developments in 1972. After a spell in receivership in 1974, the assets were bought by a consortium. In 1977 Robin Hamilton, an Aston Martin dealer, developed the RHAM/1, based on a production DBS V-8, which made several racing appearances including a run at Le Mans in 1977. However, Hamilton closed the project in 1980 and joined forces with Victor Gauntlett, who with Greek ship owner, George Livanos, had bought the Aston Martin company in 1981.

These were the partners in Nimrod Racing, which built the Nimrod-Aston C2 using a Lola-built chassis and the company's V-8 engine. The C2 was raced in 1982 and 1983. Seventh place was gained at Le Mans in 1982, among average results which that year placed the team third in the World Endurance Racing Championship. Nimrod closed down at the end of the 1983 season.

The next team to take up the Aston Martin cause was EMKA, sponsored by Steve O'Rourke, the manager of the Pink Floyd rock group. The EMKA had a chassis designed by Ford man, Len Bailey, who had had much to do with the successful Ford racing programme of the 1960s, and used a V-8 engine. It had the distinction of being the first British car to finish at Le Mans in 1983 and 1985 albeit in 17th and 11th places respectively.

Victor Gauntlett sold his interest to the Livanos family in 1983 but stayed on as chief executive to witness the sale of a controlling interest in the company to the Ford Motor Company in 1987. The 1989 season saw a semi-official return to racing when Gauntlett joined forces with Peter Livanos to sponsor the AML1. This had a carbon-

Martin 1-2-3 in the Tourist Trophy, now at Goodwood.

Nineteen fifty-nine was the *annus mirabilis* for Aston Martin and the DBR1. Moss and Jack Fairman won for a third time at the Nürburgring, then came the victory for which David Brown had worked for so long. Roy Salvadori and Carroll Shelby came first at Le Mans. The season finished with Moss, Shelby and Fairman sharing the winning car in the Tourist Trophy. These victories brought the World Sports Car Constructors' Championship to Aston Martin.

After contesting international sports car races at the top level for ten seasons, Aston Martin announced that it was withdrawing from that branch of the sport, but another venture was already under way. David Brown had his eye on Formula 1. As a taster, a single-seater DB3S had been raced by Reg Parnell in the New Zealand winter series in 1956. In 1957 three full GP cars, the DBR4s, were built, but as the team was fully engaged in sports car racing, they were put to one side.

The DBR4s finally came out in 1959 but were already obsolete. In 1957 they could have been competitive, but two years later a new generation of lightweight rear-engined GP cars had arrived. The DBR4s raced in 1959 and 1960 but with no chance of success.

fibre/Kevlar monocoque chassis designed by Max Boxstrom and a development of the Virage V-8 engine enlarged to 6.0 litres and fitted with four-valve cylinder heads.

Intended to be a serious long-term venture, in its first season the AML1 managed a fourth place in the Endurance Championship race at Brands Hatch, but Ford looked hard at the accounts and stopped the venture at the end of 1989. Ford's attitude changed during the next decade. In 2003 a return to racing was sanctioned with the DBR9, a racing version of the production V-12 DB9, which competed in the GT class.

In 2005 the DBR9 won the GT class in the Sebring 12-hour race and went on to score a 1-2 in the Tourist Trophy at Silverstone. The venture paid off handsomely in 2007 when a green-painted DBR9 won the GT class at Le Mans driven by David Brabham, Rick Rydell and Darren Turner. It was a memorable win, because in some respects the GT competitors are more in tune with the original Le Mans concept than the extreme sports-racers competing for outright victory. On and off, Aston Martin have been wearing the green for 87 years; a truly honourable record.

Roy Salvadori beating the GTO Ferraris at Monza with the DP214 in 1963.

The DBR9 which finished in 9th place at Le Mans in 2006.

CHAPTER 8

Noble Ventures: Austin, Lagonda and Riley

AUSTIN, Lagonda and Riley flourished notably in motor racing between the two World Wars. First in alphabetical priority, Herbert Austin founded the Austin Motor Company at Longbridge, outside Birmingham, in 1905. He already had racing experience as he had designed the Wolseley which he drove in the 1902 Gordon Bennett race. In 1908 Austin designed and built a team of cars for the French Grand Prix at Dieppe with 9.6-litre six-cylinder engines. Although not fast enough to challenge for the lead, two finished in 15th and 16th places.

From 1908 until 1914 Austin had many successes at Brooklands, notably with a tuned and developed 25/30 hp tourer known as 'Pobble'. Among 'Pobble's drivers was Muriel Thompson, the first woman to win a race at the track. In 1922 the soon-to-be-legendary Austin Seven small car was introduced and the company began a racing programme for it immediately. The Seven's first racing appearance was at Shelsley Walsh in 1922 and in 1923 the Seven was raced by several drivers at Brooklands.

A racing car based on the standard production car was prepared under the supervision of Capt. Arthur Waite, Herbert Austin's son-in-law. In May 1923 Waite took this car to Monza for the Gran Premio Cyclecars and won the 750 cc class easily. From then it was victory all the way with very few setbacks. The Seven dominated the 750 cc class in sprints, hill climbs and at Brooklands meetings. There were class wins in the JCC 200-Miles, the longest race being held in England.

The Seven was ideal for the enthusiast who wanted to race on a limited budget. Independent tuners began to market sporting versions, notably Gordon England who produced the Brooklands model, guaranteed to do 75 mph. At the opening meeting of the new track at Montlhéry in October 1924 Sevens took the first four places in the 75-mile race, led by Gordon England, the four finishing only 1.2 seconds apart. After this meeting England stayed on and broke 19 class records.

With some Sevens supercharged in 1925, success continued with the expected class win in the 200-Miles and many wins in lesser races at Brooklands, while in Spain Ignazio Zubiaga won the 750 cc class of the G.P. de San Sebastian. It was much the same in 1926, but a more ambitious Zubiaga took third place in the 1,100 cc class of the Targa Florio, a huge test for a small car. It was the same story in 1926 and 1927. In the latter year, in the first Brooklands long-distance sports car race, the Essex Six-Hours, a Seven driven by J.P. Dingle finished the race and inevitably won its class.

At the end of 1927 the company decided to develop its own sports Seven. The outcome was the supercharged Super Sports model which later evolved into the famous Ulster. Arthur Waite took a prototype to Australia and won the first Australian Grand Prix in March 1928, while Dingle came out again for the 1928 Six-Hours and took second place on handicap. The Austin was being built in Germany as the Dixi, later to evolve into the BMW, and these had several successes at the Avus, the Nürburgring and in the long continental hill climbs.

The Super Sports earned its Ulster sobriquet in 1929 when Archie Frazer-Nash – who had forsaken the cars he had been making – took a Seven into third place in the Ulster Tourist Trophy. At the end of the 1929 season the first BRDC 500-Mile race was held at Brooklands; it was a handicap and a Seven won the 1,100 cc class. The Seven's biggest win came in 1930. An Ulster ran in the Double-Twelve at Brooklands in May, driven by Waite and the Earl of March. It took the *Autocar* Cup for the index of performance based on price.

The consummate triumph came in the 1930 BRDC 500, in which an orange-painted blown Ulster driven by motoring journalist Sammy Davis with Lord March was uncatchable and came home first at a remarkable average of 83.41 mph. Much was made of the son of a duke being the winner. To Davis's delight he was described in one press report as March's man-servant!

In 1931 the new C-type MG was too quick for the Ulster, but there was a little-publicised success when an Ulster, driven by Italian Bruno Trevisan and works driver Charles Goodacre, came second in the 1,100 cc class of the gruelling Mille Miglia over 1,000 miles of Italian open roads.

Longbridge now concentrated on single-seat racers, though a team of three Ulsters won the LCC Relay Race at Brooklands. The first single-seaters were now known as 'Rubber Ducks', thanks to their jaunty looks. With one of these Lord March won a heat of the 1932 British Empire Trophy. In May 1932 a 'Duck' went to Berlin's Avus where, driven by Donald Barnes, it came second overall in the 1,500 cc race.

Engaged by Austin to develop the single-seaters, engineer Murray Jamieson came up with a new car which was a considerable advance on the 'Ducks'. Although fast, it was not able to match the MGs. Sir Herbert (later Lord) Austin gave Jamieson a free hand to design and build a new car aimed to be unequivocally the fastest 750 of all.

Jamieson's design had nothing in common with previous Sevens. It was an out-and-out racing car with a special chassis and a supercharged twin-cam four-cylinder engine. After the inevitable teething problems the new Austin was unbeatable in its class and gained many successes at Brooklands, Donington and the Crystal Palace. The greatest success was a win by Charlie Dodson in the 1937 British Empire Trophy at Donington. Bert Hadley had the distinction of winning the Imperial Trophy at the Crystal Palace, the last race meeting in England before World War Two began.

The 1908 Grand Prix Austin.

Lord March and Sammy Davis with their Ulster Austin after winning the 1930 BRDC 500-Mile race at Brooklands.

The twin-cam Austins were reputedly paid for wholly by Lord Austin, a costly venture which produced remarkable cars that regrettably were never raced again. In 1952 Austin became part of the British Motor Corporation. There was a final flurry of racing activity before the marque was virtually submerged by a tsunami of badge engineering. In 1958 Jack Sears won the British Touring Car Championship in an A105 Austin saloon. Two years later, in 1960, Dr. George Shepherd, a Cambridgeshire physician – old enough to be the father of most of his fellow competitors – won the Championship again in an Austin A40. The Mini was badged as an Austin, but that story is told elsewhere.

At the other end of the scale in size and price from Austin was Lagonda. Appearing in 1904, the first Lagonda was built by Wilbur Gunn, an expatriate American. The company's factory at Staines, west of London, initially made light cars. Its first major

competition venture was the appearance of a pair of racing versions of the current 11.9 hp touring car which ran, without distinction, in the 1921 and 1922 200-mile races at Brooklands.

During the 1920s the Lagonda grew into a sporting 2.0-litre tourer, a team of three of which ran at Le Mans in 1928, one finishing 11th. In 1929 the management of the team was taken over by Fox & Nicholl, a firm of motor dealers and engineers at Tolworth, not far from Brooklands. The 2.0-litre cars ran at Brooklands in the Double-Twelve, gaining a class win. A single car retired at Le Mans and in the Brooklands Six-Hour race a new model, the 3.0 litre, won its class.

A parting of the ways came in 1930 when Fox & Nicholl took over the management of Talbot's racing affairs. Thereafter there was little racing activity until 1934. The direction of Lagonda had changed. Its cars were now bigger, using the 4½-litre six-cylinder Meadows, a rugged proprietary engine. Fox & Nicholl came back into the frame after Talbot withdrew from racing, preparing a team of three Lagonda M45s for the 1934

Tourist Trophy. These finished 4th, 5th and 8th. The fourth-placed car driven by the Hon. Brian Lewis had contended for the lead during the race.

With Lagonda in financial difficulties, in April 1935 a receiver was appointed. Meanwhile Arthur Fox of Fox & Nicholl had entered two M45s for Le Mans. One of these, driven by Luis Fontes, an Anglo-Brazilian and John Hindmarsh, a Hawker test pilot, pulled off an unexpected victory, seeing off a strong challenge from Alfa Romeo. The victory helped the receiver in his quest for a buyer for the ailing company, a sale being completed a few days later to Alan Good, a London solicitor.

There were ironic postscripts to the win. A few months later Fontes went to prison for three years after a hit-and-run accident. He lost his life during World War Two as a pilot with Air Transport Auxiliary. Hindmarsh had been killed testing a Hawker Hurricane in 1938.

Alan Good engaged W.O. Bentley to refine the Meadows engine and start work on a new design. The M45s raced in 1936 but there was no great success;

The 750 cc twin-cam Austin in the Donington pits in 1939.

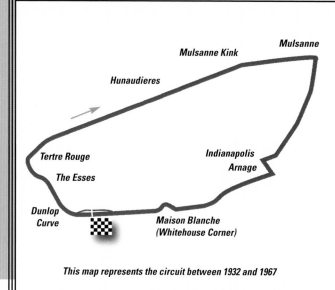

Mulsanne

Mulsanne Kink

Hunaudieres

Tertre Rouge

Indianapolis

Arnage

The Esses

Dunlop
Curve

Maison Blanche
(Whitehouse Corner)

This map represents the circuit between 1932 and 1967

L E MANS and its 24-hour race, the Grand Prix d'Endurance to give its full title, has been a magnet for British drivers since the race was first run in 1923. The racing history of Le Mans began earlier as it was the venue for the first French G.P. in 1906, though this was held on a 64-mile circuit outside the town. The Sarthe circuit over local roads on which the 24-hour race is held was first used in 1921 for the French G.P.

Since the first 24-hour race the circuit has been changed many times. Originally it ran into the outskirts of the city but this section was lopped off in 1929 and changed again in 1933. The narrow tree-lined and rough road was gradually replaced by a wide superbly surfaced track. The original open pits became a huge multi-storey construction and permanent grandstands were built. As the speeds of the cars rose in the latter years of the 20th century, artificial chicanes were introduced. Few traces of the original course remain.

A shorter version, the Bugatti circuit, which uses the main pits was built in the 1960s and was used for the 1967 French G.P. Le Mans has been the scene of many great British triumphs. The reputations of many British manufacturers have been made there.

A 2.0-litre Lagonda at Le Mans in 1929.

then Bentley came out with a remarkable engine, a 4½-litre V-12 to which Stewart Tresilian also contributed. This went into the road cars while two V-12s were prepared for racing and ran at Le Mans in 1939. Keeping to strict rev limits the cars finished 3rd and 4th, but World War Two ended hopes of success in 1940. The V-12 did not race again.

When Lagonda was bought by David Brown in 1948, included in the sale was the 2.6-litre Lagonda engine which Bentley and Willie Watson had designed for the post-war range. In 1954 a new 4,486 cc V-12 engine was designed by Watson and fitted into a chassis with similarities to the DB3S Aston Martin. This ran at Le Mans in 1954 and 1955 but was a failure, with many technical problems. After that Lagonda raced no more.

Returning to the smaller categories, Coventry's Riley first made an impression in motor racing with its 11.9 hp 'Redwing' which won races at Brooklands in the early and mid-1920s. The introduction of the four-cylinder 1,089 cc Nine in 1926 set the company on the road to real success. With two camshafts set high in the cylinder block and a hemispherical combustion chamber, the engine was an ideal unit to tune.

A Nine converted into a racing car by Parry Thomas and Reid Railton became the ultra-low sports Brooklands model. Appearing in 1928, the Brooklands immediately

gained class wins in the long-distance sports car races at Brooklands and in the Tourist Trophy. The first continental success came in July 1931 when Dudley Froy won the 1,100 cc class of the German G.P. on the Nürburgring, beating the C6 Amilcar of José Scaron, then regarded as the European 1,100 cc class champion.

The 4½-litre M45 Lagonda, which won the 1935 Le Mans 24-hour race, at the pits before the start.

The 1939 Le Mans V-12 Lagonda.

Sammy Davis makes a pit stop with his Brooklands-model Riley in the 1929 Ulster Tourist Trophy.

Freddie Dixon in one of his special Rileys during the 1934 Mannin Moar in the Isle of Man.

by Freddie Dixon. A notably successful motorcycle racer, Dixon now devoted himself to tuning Rileys. Working on the Nine and on the newly introduced 1.5-litre and 2.0-litre sixes, he produced remarkable outputs from these unsupercharged engines.

In 1933 Dixon beat the supercharged K3 MGs to win the Mannin Beg in the Isle of Man while a Brooklands won the Index of Performance at Le Mans driven by Peacock and von der Becke. A 1½-litre Six scored its first success by winning its class in the Tourist Trophy. The Six that was handed to Raymond Mays during 1933 became the 'White Riley' from which the ERA was developed.

At Le Mans in 1934 Riley's 1½-litre ixes came second and third. The second-place car, driven by the French pair Sébilleau and Delaroche, was almost within sight of outright victory when the winning Alfa Romeo struggled to the finish with a badly leaking fuel tank. It was the highest placing ever achieved by a 1.5-litre car at Le Mans. Peacock and von der Becke won the Index again and also took the coveted Rudge Whitworth Cup. At the end of the 1934 season Dixon's development of the Six bore fruit, as he won the BRDC 500-Mile race at Brooklands with a 2.0-litre version.

A new sports model, the Sprite, appeared in 1935 with a 1½-litre four-cylinder engine. A racing version won the 1935 Tourist Trophy driven by Dixon, who had already led home a Riley 1-2-3 in the British Empire Trophy at

The first major outright win came in May 1932 when a Brooklands driven by Elsie Wisdom and Joan Richmond won the 1,000-mile race at Brooklands. In September 1932 Cyril Whitcroft gained victory in the Tourist Trophy. A Brooklands was driven in the Tourist Trophy

Brooklands. At the end of the season a 2.0 litre came second in the BRDC 500. When in 1936 the French G.P. was run as a sports car race, TT Sprites took the first four places in the 2.0-litre class, seeing off both Aston Martin and 328 BMW competition. Dixon took a TT Sprite to a second Tourist Trophy win and finished off the 1936 season by winning the BRDC 500 in a 2.0 litre.

Riley was feeling the financial pinch as its over-wide range of production saloons and touring cars was uneconomic, so its racing programme was cut back in 1937. There was a 1-2-3 in the supporting 1,500 cc race for the French G.P. and another second place in the BRDC 500. After that the only major successes were gained by Percy Maclure driving a development car with independent front suspension and a variety of engines in British races. Maclure won the JCC International Trophy at Brooklands in 1938, beating the ERAs.

After Riley was taken over by the Nuffield group in 1938 all racing activity ceased. Rileys continued to gain many successes with private owners in the immediate post-war years. Mike Hawthorn began the career which was to lead to the 1958 World Championship when he raced an Ulster Imp and a TT Sprite in 1951, prepared by his father Leslie.

When Nuffield was absorbed into the British Motor Corporation, the name lived on in the 1.5 saloon which was raced extensively in touring-car events in the late 1950s and early 1960s, although the car bore no relationship to the great pre-war racers. When 1.5 production ended, a great and most successful name disappeared from the international circuits for ever, although Rileys are still major players in vintage racing. The Riley marque is now lodged with BMW, which from time to time has flirted with its revival.

A 1935/36 1½-litre Riley TT Sprite outside the Riley factory.

CHAPTER 9

Alta, HWM and Connaught:
Big Talent, Big Enthusiasm and Little Money

THESE three bearers of the green in Grand Prix racing have an important element in common: they all used the Alta engines made by Geoffrey Taylor. Taylor was born in 1903, the son of well-to-do parents who lived in a large house on Kingston Hill, south-west of London. Taylor used his notable technical skills to start a small engineering concern in the stables of his parents' house. There he did contract machining work while building a sports car from scratch.

This first Alta had a four-cylinder 1,074 cc twin-cam engine. Taylor virtually built the car from the basic metal, devising a method of powering his machine tools from the domestic water system. He finished the car in 1928. It was a low businesslike car which he drove in trials and minor speed events.

In 1931 Taylor built a small factory, which was little more than a tin shack on the Kingston Bypass, and formed the Alta Car & Engineering Co. He began producing the supercharged 1.1-litre sports Alta in very small numbers, doing almost all the work himself. About 12 cars were built between 1931 and 1935, all going to enthusiasts. Nearly all were raced at Brooklands and Donington, gaining some minor successes.

By 1935 Taylor had enlarged the engine to 1.5 litres and then to 2.0 litres. It went into the sports car and also into an offset single-seater racing car. Taylor made six of these which had a reputation for being quick, especially the 2.0-litre version, albeit unreliable.

At the beginning of 1937 Taylor built a new single-seater which had all-independent suspension. It was bought by Philip Jucker, an erratic driver who was killed when he crashed it during practice for its first race. The wreck was sold to George Abecassis, who had rich parents, ran a garage as a hobby in West London and had raced an Austin Seven. He raced the rebuilt Alta in British events in 1938 and 1939, being particularly successful at the Crystal Palace. He also gained wins with a 2.0-litre sports Alta.

As soon as World War Two ended Taylor announced plans for a new 1½-litre GP, eligible for the Grand Prix Formula 1 coming into force in 1947. It had the developed pre-war supercharged four-cylinder engine in a tubular chassis with independent suspension using rubber blocks as a springing medium. Finished in 1948, the light metallic-green first car was sold to Abecassis, but was disappointing. He abandoned it at the end of 1949. Two other similar cars were built but achieved nothing.

Taylor also built five unsupercharged 2.0-litre single seaters in 1951 and 1952 for the subsidiary Formula 2, but these too achieved minimal results. The builder was in no position to test and develop his cars, a task he left up to the owners, who similarly were not able to take on such a difficult task. If an entrant with the determination and resources of Rob Walker had taken up the Alta cause, it might have been different.

At the end of World War Two Abecassis, who had been a decorated bomber pilot and spent two years as a prisoner of war, joined forces with John Heath, who had an engineering business at Hersham, not far from Brooklands. They founded HW Motors at Walton-on-Thames, also adjacent to the old Brooklands site. As well as running an ordinary commercial garage, they began an active racing programme using a sports Alta, an ERA, a Type 59 Bugatti and the new GP Alta.

Heath concentrated on the sports Alta, in 1948 building an all-enveloping bodied sports car using Alta components which lived up to the established Alta reputation of being fast but unreliable. In 1949 Heath built a new car, the HW-Alta, which was intended to be a dual-purpose F2/sports-racing car. It had an unsupercharged 2.0-litre Alta engine and a chassis made largely from proprietary components.

With his HW-Alta, Heath won the F2 Manx Cup in the Isle of Man and was well placed in other F2 events.

Then in July of 1949 he drove the car, fitted with road equipment, across France to Comminges for the French G.P. which was being run as a sports car race. To the amazement of the French drivers, the HW-Alta came second ahead of seemingly much faster cars.

During the winter of 1949-50 Heath and Abecassis built four cars, developments of the HW-Alta which were called HWM. Like the earlier car, these had a two-seat body and a 2.0-litre Alta engine. One car was sold to a private owner and the other three were retained as a team, the aim being to run the cars in F2 events all over Europe. This offered the possibility of having a race almost every weekend throughout the season.

Heath and Abecassis shared the driving of one car while the second would be loaned or hired to a local driver and the third went to a remarkable newcomer, 20-year-old Stirling Moss, who had dominated the new class of 500 cc racing in the 1949 season. In the immediate post-war years British drivers racing in Europe had been treated as a joke, with outdated cars and amateurish organisation, but the HWM team showed a new face of British racing.

Painted a light metallic-green, the HWMs were well-prepared and never failed to appear for every event for which they were entered; the team soon became a regular

The 1,100 cc Alta of A.C. Lace passes the stranded R-type MG of George Eyston in the 1935 Mannin Beg.

George Abecassis in his 1937 independently sprung 1,500 cc Alta at Prescott hill climb.

Abecassis in the 1948 GP Alta during the 1949 British Grand Prix.

and respected member of the F2 'circus'. There was only one win, in the G.P. des Frontieres in Belgium, but there were several places with Moss showing that he could race on level terms with the all-conquering Ferrari F2 team. HWM was invited to run in the full F1 race at Bari in Italy where Moss came a stellar third behind the Type 158 Alfa Romeos of Fangio and Farina, with more than twice the power, and in front of the rest of the field of Ferraris and Maseratis.

For the 1951 season a team of four single-seaters was built. Many of the chassis components came from proprietary sources, but the Alta engine was still used and developed to give more power. Moss and Abecassis were joined by Lance Macklin and the fourth car was loaned or hired out. The team's reputation was such that even drivers of the calibre of Louis Chiron, the French Champion of the 1930s, were happy to take the wheel.

There were no outright wins, except when the team made occasional appearances in minor English races, but a profitable string of second and third places in European F2 races was scored. The cars were capable of finishing in front of all the private entrants when invited to compete in F1 races.

The 1951 season was the high point of HWM's fortunes. At the end of the season Stirling Moss and Alf Francis, the team's chief mechanic, suggested that the 1951 cars should be developed and improved, with more power being found from the Alta engines. Heath, however, was determined to build new cars and so Moss and Francis left the team.

The new cars were an improvement, but the former F2 class had been promoted and was now the class for the World Championship. Many cars, especially the Italians, were faster than the HWMs. Despite the talents of Peter Collins, who had replaced Moss, there were only two wins, in the G.P. des Frontieres and in the International Trophy at Silverstone.

More new cars were built for 1953 but were even less competitive. When the new 2½-litre Grand Prix formula was introduced in 1954, an Alta engine was expanded to 2½ litres and fitted to one of the 1953 chassis, but the car was hopelessly outclassed. That was the end for the HWM single-seaters.

A series of sports-racing HWMs were built using adapted single-seater chassis and Jaguar engines. The HWM-Jaguars were very successful in British club and national events, although the results in long-distance European races were disappointing. In 1956 John Heath took the latest HWM-Jaguar to Italy to compete in the Mille Miglia. Sadly he crashed and died of his injuries. His death effectively brought the racing activities of the HWM team to an end. Although there had been no major victories or great glory, the team had raised British prestige immeasurably.

While Abecassis and Heath were establishing HW Motors in 1946, a few miles away at Ripley another company, Continental Cars Ltd., was being set up by Rodney Clarke and Michael Oliver. Their intention was to specialise in Bugatti, with racing car preparation as a sideline, but it soon became evident that there would be no

John Heath returns to the paddock after winning the 1949 Manx Cup in his 2.0-litre HWM Alta.

The HWM team lines up in front of the pits at the 1950 Swiss Grand Prix. Alf Francis who was responsible for much of the work on the cars is in no.12.

Rodney Clarke in the Lea-Francis based sports Connaught at Goodwood in 1949.

Stirling Moss in the single-seater HWM at Goodwood in 1951.

Dennis Poore in a 1952 A-type Connaught.

1949 and gained some success in minor races. However McAlpine wanted to have an F2 car so Clarke agreed to design and build a car using a highly modified Lea-Francis engine. This went into an advanced chassis which had excellent handling and roadholding and was superbly made, with a finish that was as good as any contemporary.

The first A-type Formula 2 Connaught made its racing debut in a minor race at Castle Combe in October 1950 and came second behind Moss's HWM. The A-type was raced in minor events in 1951 as a development car, after which a production run of eight cars was laid down. The A-type first came into the limelight at the 1952 British G.P. when Dennis Poore held third place for much of the race against the virtually unbeatable team of 500 F2 Ferraris and finished fourth after a delayed pit stop when he was given brake fluid to drink instead of orange juice!

For 1953 the works A-types were fitted with American Hilborn-Travers fuel injection which increased the power, though the pushrod Lea-Francis engine was still well behind the Italian teams in terms of output. The best result was second and third places in the International Trophy at Silverstone.

When the 2½ litre formula was announced, Rodney Clarke produced a revolutionary rear-engine design which anticipated the universal adoption of this layout in F1 by six years. The design was built around a proposed V-8 Coventry Climax engine, which regrettably was shelved

post-war Bugattis and so Clarke decided to build his own sports cars based on production Lea-Francis parts.

An 8CM Maserati had been prepared for Kenneth McAlpine, who was a member of the building and construction family. McAlpine agreed to fund the production of the sports cars were which were given the name 'Connaught'. The sports Connaught appeared in

Tony Brooks (left) celebrates with Stirling Moss after winning the 1957 British Grand Prix.

TONY BROOKS

Tony Brooks had no thought of becoming a professional racing driver. He was a dental student who raced as a pastime in club events, where his talent was noticed. He was recruited into the Aston Martin team in 1955. Brooks's big break came when he beat the Maserati team in the Syracuse G.P. with a Connaught to score the first British Grand Prix win for 33 years.

For 1956 Tony Brooks was snapped up by BRM, whose fast but erratic cars suffered mechanical failures and crashes from which he had fortunate escapes. Joining Vanwall in 1957, he shared the winning car with Stirling Moss in the British G.P. to gain the first British *Grande Epreuve* win since 1924.

Appreciating Brooks's talent, Juan Fangio tipped him as the man most likely to succeed him as World Champion. The 1958 season saw Tony take wins for Vanwall in Belgium, Germany and Italy to help gain the Constructors' title for the team. In 1958 he also shared victory in the Tourist Trophy with Moss, driving a DBR1 Aston Martin.

When Vanwall withdrew from racing, Tony Brooks moved to Ferrari for 1959. He won the French and German G.Ps and was World Championship runner-up. That was the last of his big years. In 1960 he drove a Cooper-Climax for the private Yeoman Credit team, then rejoined BRM in 1961, when the British teams were outclassed. The modest and immensely talented Brooks retired at the end of that season.

SILVERSTONE was a bomber airfield during World War Two. It opened as a racing circuit in 1948 with the British Grand Prix, using the perimeter track and parts of the runways. The G.P. was held there in 1949, still using the perimeter track/runway course, but in August 1949 the BRDC International Trophy used the perimeter track alone which made a faster and more practical circuit of 2.92 miles.

From 1948 until 1951 the pits were sited between Abbey Curve and Woodcote Corner. These were moved to their present position between Woodcote and Copse Corner in 1952. Until 1952 club meetings were held on a circuit using the back leg from Copse to Stowe Corner and a central runway, but since then the club circuit, now the National circuit, has used the main pit straight and a return leg to Woodcote.

After being run at Silverstone through 1954, the British G.P. was held there in alternate years, sharing the event with Aintree and Brands Hatch, until 1987. Since then Silverstone has been the home of the Grand Prix and many other major races.

After the many changes since 1948, little of the original airfield can be seen apart from the runways, which are still used for race-weekend movements. The first change was the realignment of Woodcote Corner in 1987. During a major redesign in 1991 the Luffield/Brooklands complex of corners was added and the Stowe/Club section was changed. Since 1994 there have been more minor changes.

There are now four Silverstone circuits. The full G.P. circuit is 3.19 miles while the National circuit is 1.64 miles (2.64 km). The International circuit of 2.24 miles is used for some sports and touring car races and there is the short Stowe circuit for testing.

Silverstone was leased from the Ministry of Defence by the Royal Automobile Club until 1952, when the lease was taken over by the British Racing Drivers Club. The BRDC bought the circuit outright from the Ministry in 1972. An industrial park adjoining the circuit has become a centre for many companies connected with motor racing. including F1 teams.

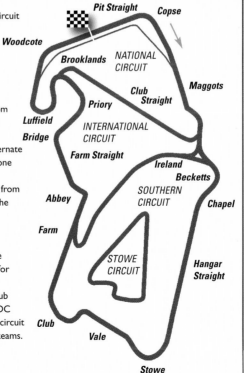

as Coventry Climax believed erroneously that their unit was producing insufficient power to be competitive.

As a stopgap Clarke had designed a front-engined car, the B-type, which was fitted with an Alta engine enlarged by Geoffrey Taylor to 2½ litres and developed by Clarke to its maximum potential. The B-type was not ready to race until 1955, when the initial results were disappointing with the cars retiring with various minor faults. Initially the B-type was fitted with an all-enveloping aerodynamic body, but it was found that although this produced gains in terms of speed it was vulnerable to damage and made the cars difficult to work on, and so it was abandoned in favour of a conventional open-wheeled body towards the end of the 1955 season.

G.P. racing in 1955 had been dominated by the W196 Mercedes-Benz team, but in October there was a non-Championship F1 race at Syracuse in Sicily. Two works B-types were entered but the team's regular drivers were not available. Tony Brooks, a dental student who had been impressive in club racing and had been given two drives in a works Aston Martin, was invited to drive. To the astonishment of the Italian teams, Brooks ran away with the race and scored the first victory by a British Grand Prix car for 30 years.

Accordingly prospects looked good for 1956, but Kenneth McAlpine was losing interest and the team ran under a cloud of uncertainty all season. The engines were reliable if nursed but if pushed to their maximum showed fragility. The best results were a fourth by Jack Fairman in the British G.P. and a third by Ron Flockhart in the Italian G.P. at Monza. Clarke designed a new chassis, the C-type, for 1957, but it did not race and the team began the season with its B-types.

A new driver, Stuart Lewis-Evans, won a minor race at the Goodwood Easter meeting, then came fourth in the Monaco G.P, but McAlpine was unwilling to put up any more money so the cars were withdrawn from racing. The whole team was auctioned piecemeal in the autumn of 1957 and a brave venture had ended.

A year later the British dominance of F1 began and in the glorious years since then, the efforts of Geoffrey Taylor, John Heath, George Abecassis, Rodney Clarke, Mike Oliver and Kenneth McAlpine have been almost forgotten. They deserve to be remembered and honoured for they played a major part in laying the foundations of the British motor racing industry.

The B-type Connaught which won the 1955 Syracuse Grand Prix.

CHAPTER 10

BRM: Failure to Triumph... to Failure

WORLD WAR TWO stopped play soon after Raymond Mays and Peter Berthon parted company with Humphrey Cook, who had joined them in co-founding ERA. During the war the resourceful and persistent Mays started a project to build a British car that would be able to compete successfully in Grand Prix racing in the post-war years.

Mays persuaded a number of firms in the British motor industry to join a consortium to fund the construction of a car to be called British Racing Motor or BRM. They were to contribute equally in cash and kind, making parts for the cars. Unfortunately, the project was under-funded at a time of soaring inflation that eroded budgets and was also 'run by committee', the BRM Trust.

The car was designed by Peter Berthon, who had grandiose ideas but lacked engineering perception. He and Eric Richter designed a 1,500 cc V-16 engine which had Rolls-Royce two-stage centrifugal superchargers and installed it in a chassis which had much in common with pre-war German practice.

With much of the support coming in the form of parts and components, in the difficult economic climate of the immediate post-war years, the BRM's backers found that this had a lesser priority than the need to survive, so although the project had been initiated before World War Two ended, the first car was not finished until the winter of 1949.

From the beginning it was evident that Berthon's design was over-complicated and under-engineered. As well, the BRM organisation, operating in the former ERA workshops behind Mays's house at Bourne, lacked the facilities and resources to make the car effective, although in order to promote the project and attract industry backing it was hailed as an almost certain world-beater.

The first car was demonstrated to the British public at the European G.P. at Silverstone in May 1950, although it was still not ready to race. Pressure from the public and the consortium forced an entry at the International Trophy at Silverstone in August 1950. Driven by the French ace Raymond Sommer, it failed on the starting line when a universal joint broke. Disappointed and frustrated spectators threw pennies into the cockpit of the broken car.

A month later the BRM won two minor races at Goodwood, driven by Reg Parnell. Two cars were run in the G.P. do Penya Rhin at Barcelona, driven by Parnell and Peter Walker. Both retired and were not competitive. The cars appeared again halfway through the 1951 season when Parnell and Walker drove in the British G.P. at

Raymond Mays in 1976 with the BRM V-16.

RAYMOND MAYS

Raymond Mays was the power behind two of Britain's great racing projects. Born in 1899, he began racing in the 1920s. Specialising in hill climbs, his AC, Bugatti and Vauxhall Villiers were the cars to beat. In 1933 he became the co-founder of ERA with Humphrey Cook.

Sparked by Mays's skill and enthusiasm, ERA became the leading *voiturette* racing car of the mid-1930s. Mays himself gained many wins driving an ERA both in Britain and on the Continent.

During World War Two Mays worked hard to form a consortium of manufacturing firms aimed at building a successful British Grand Prix contender. Backed by British motor companies, the BRM was the outcome. Despite countless setbacks and failures, Mays never lost faith in his venture and was rewarded when BRM won the F1 Constructors' title in 1962.

Raymond Mays gradually reduced his involvement with BRM and died in 1980. His many years of striving for British prestige in motor racing were recognised when he was appointed a CBE in 1978.

Silverstone, finishing in fifth and seventh places. This was the only appearance of the V-16 BRM in a World Championship race. In 1952 the cars became obsolete when the FIA decided that the 2.0-litre F2 class should decide the World Championship.

The V-16s continued to appear in minor British events. With its mission vitiated by the switch to Formula 2 the Trust moved to wind the project up. In November 1952 it sold all the assets of BRM to Sir Alfred Owen and his Rubery Owen industrial group

Raymond Sommer in the V-16 BRM at its ill-fated Silverstone debut in 1950.

for £23,500. Owen had been a keen member of the original consortium.

BRM began to plan for the new unblown 2½ litre formula which began in 1954. Peter Berthon had been joined by Stuart Tresilian who designed a four-cylinder engine, the P25, which went into a small, neat chassis, the Type 25, which was of semi-monocoque construction. True to BRM form the car was not ready until the latter part of 1955. In minor races at Aintree and Oulton Park it showed great potential.

For 1956 BRM signed up drivers of top quality, Mike Hawthorn and Tony Brooks, but the season was a disaster. The cars were quicker than the rest of the F1 field but unreliable, with brake and chassis failures that caused serious accidents from which both drivers were lucky to escape. Halfway through the season Alfred Owen directed that the cars should not race until the problems had been overcome.

The 1957 season began inauspiciously, but the thrusting French champion, Jean Behra, was impressed with the performance of the car and borrowed one for the minor G.P. de Caen. Behra won and went on to head a BRM 1-2-3 in the International Trophy at Silverstone at the end of the season, the second and third cars being

V-16 complexity; the BRM engine.

driven by Franco-American Harry Schell and Scot Ron Flockhart.

Behra and Schell became the regular drivers in 1958 when the chassis was redesigned as a pure space frame, but niggling problems still precluded success. The best result was a second and third in the Dutch G.P. at Zandvoort. In 1959 a car was loaned to the British Racing Partnership and driven by Stirling Moss in some races, but the Swedish driver Jo Bonnier had the best result, as at last a BRM won a World Championship race, the Dutch G.P. Moss's best result was a second in the British G.P. at Aintree.

The rear-engined revolution had come to Grand Prix racing. BRM responded remarkably quickly, thanks to the initiative of ex-Rolls-Royce engineer Tony Rudd. At the end of 1959 the Type 25 parts were reworked into a rear-engined car, the P48. Bonnier was joined in the team by the American driver Dan Gurney, in his second G.P. season, and by Graham Hill. The P48 showed promise with Hill leading the British G.P. until the brakes failed, but a third at Zandvoort was the best that could be shown.

In 1961 the Grand Prix Formula 1 changed to 1,500 cc unsupercharged. The British manufacturers opposed the change and hoped that their resistance would

Jo Bonnier gains the first Championship win for BRM with the P25 in the 1959 Dutch Grand Prix.

BRM had tried semi-monocoque construction with its Type 25. The success Lotus had with this method in the Lotus 25 in 1962 and 1963 made Rudd realise it should be used again, a prototype coming out during 1963. For 1964 a pure monocoque, the P261, appeared, using the V-8 engine. Though Hill seemed likely to win the 1964 Championship he was nudged off the track in the last round in Mexico. Under the scoring system only the best eight results counted, so he had to discard his worst score and the Championship went to Ferrari-mounted John Surtees by one point. Hill won at Monaco and in the United States and also picked up three second places. Once again BRM was the runner-up in the Constructors' Championship.

For 1966 the Grand Prix Formula 1 was changing to 3.0-litres unsupercharged and 1.5-litres blown. Looking ahead, realising that the new cars would be more powerful, BRM built a four-wheel-drive prototype. It was tested but never raced, though it took the 1968 British Hill Climb Championship driven by Peter Lawson.

For the last 1.5-litre season, 1965, Hill was joined by Scotsman Jackie Stewart who had made a huge impression racing a Cooper for the Tyrrell team in F3 during 1964. The P261 continued, Hill scoring a third win at Monaco and also winning in the United States again. This was popular because the Watkins Glen race was the season's most financially rewarding. Stewart showed his form with three second places and a win in the Italian G.P at Monza. These results took Hill and Stewart to second and third in the Drivers' Championship while once again BRM was the runner-up in the Constructors' Championship.

In 1963 BRM collaborated with the Rover company, which had been experimenting with a gas turbine as a possible form of propulsion for road cars since the mid-1950s. For a Rover turbine BRM built a coupé using Type 25 and P678 components. This Rover-BRM ran at Le Mans in 1963, driven by Hill and Ginther, finishing in seventh place after a trouble free run. A neater, more shapely version ran again in 1965 with Stewart as Hill's co-driver and came 10th.

force the FIA to revert to the old formula, but the change went ahead. Thus BRM like the other British teams effectively lost a year. A stop-gap BRM, the P57, built with a four-cylinder Coventry Climax engine, lacked the power to challenge Ferrari which swept the board.

The year 1962 saw a change of fortune, bringing the results at last that the team had worked for since 1950. With Aubrey Woods as draftsman Peter Berthon designed a new V-8 1,500 cc engine. This went into a new space-frame chassis designed and developed by Tony Rudd. The new car took Graham Hill to the World Championship with wins in the Dutch, German and South African G.Ps and second places in Belgium and the United States. As well, BRM won the F1 Constructors' Championship.

With modifications the V-8 raced again in 1963, but the brilliance of Jim Clark took the Championship and Hill had only two wins at Monaco and in the United States. Consistent placings secured him second in the Championship while his team-mate Ritchie Ginther, the freckled American, was third and BRM was runner-up in the Constructors' Championship.

Ritchie Ginther in the P578 BRM at the 1962 Goodwood Easter meeting.

Ginther in the P261 BRM leads Bruce McLaren's Cooper-Climax in the 1964 French Grand Prix at Rouen.

Lighter and more compact, capable of 12,000 rpm, the costly 64-valve Mark 3 version of BRM's H-16 was revealed in 1969 but never installed in a car.

There were signs of a reversion to the old BRM inclination toward excessive hubris when a new and complicated H-16 engine was designed for the 3.0-litre formula in 1966. Supercharging the 1.5-litre V-8 had been a possibility but this avenue was not explored. As a back-up, intended for sale to sports car builders, a V-12 was also designed. Neither project was ready for the start of the new season so the P261 engines were bored out to 2.0-litres as a stopgap. One of these gave Stewart victory at Monaco.

The H-16 did not live up to the team's hopes, being excessively heavy, underpowered and unreliable. There was only one win when Clark took the United States G.P. with an H-16 which was supplied to Lotus, who were waiting for the new Ford–Cosworth DFV V-8. The H-16 went into a new bulky P83 but it produced no results and at the end of 1966 Hill left the team to go to Lotus.

Upcoming Briton Mike Spence joined Stewart in the team for 1967 and they persevered with the H-16. The best result was a second place by Stewart at Spa after he had led until suffering gear-selection bothers. He reverted to the P261 for the French G.P. at Le Mans and came third. At the end of the season a lighter P115 appeared

but made little difference and the H-16 was abandoned as a lost cause.

Hopes for 1968 now rested on the V-12, which had first raced in 1967 in a McLaren chassis. A new car, the P126, was designed by consultant Len Terry, whose firm built the first three cars. The second batch, built at Bourne, although similar, became the P133. The P126s were run as a separate team by Reg Parnell (Racing) with Piers Courage and Richard Attwood as drivers, while the Owen Organisation's team signed up Pedro Rodriguez and Mike Spence. After Spence was killed in a practice accident at Indianapolis in a gas-turbine Lotus, Attwood moved over to the Owen team. The results were modest, with second places at Monaco and Spa and a third at Zandvoort.

A new 48-valve cylinder head was fitted to the V-12 for 1969. Now the engine developed some 440 bhp, an increase of 50 bhp on the 24-valve engine. A change-round of drivers brought John Surtees, the 1964 Champion, and Jackie Oliver to the team while Pedro Rodriguez shuttled between the Owen and Parnell teams. With the new engine the cars became the P138. As well, a new chassis, the P139, was designed by Alec Osborn.

Increasing involvement in the team by Louis Stanley, husband of Alfred Owen's sister Jean, did not sit well with Tony Rudd. In mid-1969 Rudd left to join Lotus. In considerable chaos, the team could only salvage a third place by Surtees in the United States G.P. Tony Southgate, who had previously worked with Lola and Dan Gurney's All American Eagle team, was appointed as chief designer. He came up with a new design for 1970, the P153, which overcame some of the aerodynamic problems of the P138/9.

Jackie Stewart in the H-16 engined P83 BRM at the 1966 United States Grand Prix.

The era of commercial sponsorship was enthusiastically embraced by Louis Stanley. The BRMs were no longer painted dark green with an orange nose band. They appeared instead in the white, gold, brown and black livery of the new sponsor, Yardley Cosmetics. The drivers were Oliver, Rodriguez and the Canadian, George Eaton. At last there was a satisfactory result when Pedro Rodriguez won the ultra-fast Belgian G.P at Spa, though the rest of the season was disappointing, with various mechanical problems. The best was a second place gained by Rodriguez in the United States.

For 1971 Southgate produced a development of the P153, the P160. The Swiss driver, Jo Siffert, was signed up to join Rodriguez with the New Zealander, Howden Ganley, in the third seat. The P160 was competitive and Rodriguez was second at Spa, but then was killed in a sports car race and so the British F3 driver, Peter Gethin, joined the team. Siffert scored a win in the Austrian G.P at the Österreichring. Then in a dramatic slipstreaming battle at Monza for the Italian G.P, where one second covered the first five cars at the finish, Gethin was the winner. The season ended with the minor World Championship Victory Race at Brands Hatch where poor Siffert was killed when his P160 crashed and caught fire.

Nineteen seventy-one seemed to promise an upswing in BRM fortunes, the marque placing second behind Tyrrell in the Constructors' Championship. However this counted for nothing when Louis Stanley, a bombastic man with a huge ego, decided that BRM would field five cars for the 1972 season. Yardley was abandoned and a deal was signed with Marlboro tobacco. The team had been hard-stretched running three cars, so five became unmanageable.

Southgate produced the P180, an updated P160, but the handling was poor. There was only one worthwhile result, the French driver Jean-Pierre Beltoise winning at Monaco, the last BRM World Championship victory. At the end of 1972 Southgate departed. BRM had plummeted to seventh out of nine in the ranking of Grand Prix marques.

The 1973 season was no better, Marlboro pulling out at the end of the season, while the Owen Group had financial problems. It was much the same in 1974 when a second place in South Africa was all that could be shown. In 1975 the BRM team and the Owen Group parted company. Louis Stanley tried to carry on in 1976 and 1977, years of a succession of non-starts and failures to qualify. At the end of 1977 the saga came to an end. An abortive attempt to rebadge another V-12 as a BRM for sports car racing in 1992 only underlined the marque's enervation.

BRM had started with high hopes, ideals and enthusiasm. Despite a brief period of success, the organisational failures which bedevilled the project from the start were never really shaken off. It could and should have been better.

GRAHAM HILL

When BRM won the Constructors' title in 1962, the lead driver was Graham Hill who became World Champion. Hill's story was truly one of rags to riches. He began as a penniless racing mechanic. When he started working for Team Lotus in 1955, Colin Chapman noticed his ability as a test driver.

After an apprenticeship in sports cars Hill moved into the Lotus F1 team in 1958. There was little success and he moved to BRM in 1960. There were two lean years before the Championship in 1962. Championship runner-up in 1963, 1964 and 1965, the charismatic Hill was a star of British racing with his wit and humour.

Graham Hill returned to Lotus in 1967 where he had the benefit of the Lotus 49 and the DFV Cosworth engine. Team Lotus suffered a huge setback when his team-mate Jim Clark was killed at the beginning of 1968. Hill rose to the occasion. With three victories and several places he secured the World title for himself and the Constructors' title for Lotus.

After that it was downhill for a driver whose successes were gained by sheer hard graft. Hill drove for privateer Rob Walker and for Brabham between 1970 and 1972, then formed his own team. Not a success, this was beset with financial problems. It all came to an end in November 1972 when Hill was killed in an aircraft he was piloting, returning from a testing session. His great legacy to motor racing was his son Damon who was World Champion in 1996.

Pedro Rodriguez in a P153 BRM leads the Lotus of John Miles and the De Tomaso of Piers Courage in the 1970 Dutch Grand Prix. Shortly after this photograph was taken, Courage had a fatal crash.

CHAPTER 11

Vanwall: One Man's Passion

GUY ANTHONY (Tony) Vandervell was born in 1898. His father was the owner of CAV, a company that supplied electrical components to many manufacturers in the early British motor industry. He was also a substantial shareholder in the Norton motorcycle company. Young Tony Vandervell began riding a Norton in trials in 1914 and after World War One rode a Norton in the 1921 Senior TT in the Isle of Man. He also raced a Talbot with some success at Brooklands between 1921 and 1924.

Breaking away from his father and the CAV business, in the early 1930s Vandervell acquired the British licence from the American Cleveland Graphite Bronze Co. to make thin steel-shell bearings. By the start of World War Two the 'Thin Wall' bearing made by Vandervell Products Ltd, a vast advance over the old babbitt bearings, was used almost universally throughout the British car and aircraft industries.

Intensely patriotic, Vandervell had retained his interest in motor racing, so became an enthusiastic supporter of the BRM project and was a member of the board of the BRM Trust. However he became convinced that BRM was being bogged down and slowed by committee politics and decisions. He suggested that much could be learned from the acquisition of a current Grand Prix car for research.

At the end of 1948 Vandervell approached Enzo Ferrari to buy a supercharged 1,500 cc Type 125 F1 Ferrari. Initially Ferrari was unwilling to sell but Vandervell suggested that if there were no sale, the supply of Thin Wall bearings to Ferrari might dry up. A car was duly sold to Vandervell and was driven in the 1949 British GP at Silverstone by Raymond Mays. Vandervell's research department found many faults with the Ferrari and it was agreed that Maranello would supply an updated car.

Meanwhile Vandervell had despaired of the BRM project and concluded that it would never be successful. He broke his links with BRM in the spring of 1950. Ferrari delivered an unsupercharged 4½-litre Type 375 F1 to Vandervell in the spring of 1951. Modified and improved by the Vandervell engineers, this became known as the Thin Wall Special. It was raced by several top-line drivers, including Italian aces Piero Taruffi and Nino Farina, between 1951 and 1953 in *formule libre* races with great success.

Vandervell's ambition was to build a successful Grand Prix car. He set his staff working on a design for the 1952-1953 2.0-litre Formula 2. As a director of Norton he had great faith in that company's successful 500 cc motorcycle single, so the engine design became, in effect, four water-cooled racing 500 cc Manx Norton cylinders mounted on an improved Rolls-Royce B40 commercial crankcase. The chassis frame was made by Cooper and fitted with Ferrari transmission and suspension units redundant from the Thin Wall development.

Known as the Vanwall Special, the car was not ready until 1954, when the Grand Prix Formula 1 had changed to 2½ litres unsupercharged. Thus it first raced at Silverstone in May 1954 in 2.0 litre form. It was enlarged to 2.3 litres for the British G.P. in July, when Peter Collins was the driver, and by the end of the season was a full 2½ litres.

The 1954 season showed no great success but a lot had been learned. For 1955 four cars were built and Mike Hawthorn – at that time the most successful British driver in Grand Prix racing – was persuaded to leave the Ferrari team and sign up, together with Ken Wharton, who had been driving the V-16 BRM in *formule libre* races. The early races were not a success. The cars retired on each outing. Wharton crashed at Silverstone and his car was destroyed when it caught fire. After the Belgian G.P. Hawthorn left and went back to Ferrari.

For the British G.P. at Aintree in 1955, dominated by the unbeatable Mercedes-Benz team, the Franco-American driver Harry Schell had been signed to drive the Vanwall. He made a bad start and lost much time, but the spectators realised the Vanwall had real potential when Schell picked off the three cars of the Ferrari team on the fastest straight of the course, almost matching the speed of the W196 Mercedes. At the end of the season Schell showed the car's potential by winning two minor races at Snetterton and Castle Combe, beating Stirling Moss's personal 250 F Maserati.

For 1956 more power was found in the engine while Colin Chapman, who had built up a considerable reputation with his Lotus sports-racing cars, was engaged to design a new, stiffer chassis frame and revised rear suspension. At Chapman's suggestion Frank Costin, an experienced aerodynamicist, designed a new and distinctive low-drag body which owed much to aircraft practice.

Vandervell tried to sign up Stirling Moss as his number one driver but Moss decided to sign for Maserati, so Schell and French driver, Maurice Trintignant, were retained. Moss agreed to drive the Vanwall at the non-Championship International Trophy at Silverstone in May. Stunningly he ran away with the race, beating the D50 Lancia-Ferrari team led by Juan Fangio. This was a

bright day for British Racing Green – a dark hue on the Vanwalls.

In the Belgian G.P. at Spa, Schell showed that the Vanwall had the speed to match the leaders but the high-speed handling caused problems and he came fourth. Mike Hawthorn returned to Vanwall for the French G.P. at Reims. He had driven in the 12-hour sports car race which preceded the G.P. and was tired. After a few laps he handed his car over to Schell whose Vanwall had

Peter Collins in the 4½-litre Thin Wall Special Ferrari at Aintree in 1954.

*Alan Brown with the first Vanwall in the
International Trophy at Silverstone in 1954.*

*Tony Vandervell with his two cars at
Snetterton in 1955. Harry Schell is in no.142.*

Stirling Moss winning the 1956 International Trophy at Silverstone.

Tony Vandervell says a few words after Moss has won the 1956 International Trophy. Colin Chapman, the progenitor and guiding force of Lotus, who had redesigned the Vanwall chassis, is on the left.

SIR STIRLING MOSS

Sir Stirling Moss has been described as the '... greatest driver never to win a World Championship'. Perhaps he would be better described as one of the most versatile drivers of all time.

Moss was born in 1929 into a motor-sporting family. His father Alfred raced at Brooklands and in the Indy 500 in the 1920s and his mother Aileen was a leading trial and rally driver in the 1930s. Stirling began with a 328 BMW in 1947 but was one of the first customers for a Cooper 500. He dominated the 500 cc class in 1948 and 1949. He joined the F2 HWM team in 1950 and showed he had top-line talent, but his first big win was in the 1950 Tourist Trophy with an XK120 Jaguar.

While he continued to pile up sports car wins in Jaguars, the years from 1951 to 1954 were lean for Moss, who tried in vain to find British single-seaters that matched his abilities. In 1954 he went 'foreign'. With a 250 F Maserati he showed he was one of the very best in F1. His versatility emerged when he won an Alpine Cup in the most testing Alpine Rally with a Sunbeam-Talbot.

Like Dick Seaman before him, Moss was invited to join the Mercedes-Benz team. In 1955 he was the nominal number two to Fangio, but while he followed Fangio in F1 – apart from his first F1 win in the British G.P. – he was top dog with the 300 SLR Mercedes sports car. He scored a remarkable win, perhaps one of his greatest, in the Mille Miglia and also won the Tourist Trophy and the Targa Florio.

With Mercedes out, in 1956 Moss drove for Maserati. He began establishing a pattern which would remain for several seasons in which he either won in F1 or his car broke. He was back in a green car in 1957 driving for Vanwall. Staying with the British team in 1958, he lost the World Championship to Mike Hawthorn by one point and became Championship runner-up for the fourth successive season. Away from F1 he was scoring numerous wins in sports car races with Aston Martin and Maserati.

In 1959 Moss divided his F1 drives between Cooper and BRM, driving the former for Rob Walker, but mechanical failures blunted his Championship ambitions. With Aston Martin, Moss played a major part in securing the World Sports Car Championship for the British firm. After a good start in 1960 he was sidelined for most of the season after being badly hurt when the suspension of his Walker-entered Lotus failed in practice for the Belgian G.P.

Moss revelled in the role of the underdog, often beating the opposition with an inferior or underpowered car. Still with Rob Walker in 1961, he showed this quality when he defeated the Ferrari team at Monaco and the Nürburgring with a Lotus-Climax in a season when the Ferraris were otherwise unbeatable.

Stirling Moss's top-line career ended when he crashed a Lotus at the 1962 Goodwood Easter meeting and was severely injured. He subsequently made a full recovery but retired from front-line racing. Since then the dynamic and inventive Moss has been continuously active in the sport, driving in historic races, maintaining a constant interest and giving support to many ventures and initiatives. His achievements and his lifetime of patriotic support for British motor racing were recognised by his knighthood in 2000.

Moss is greeted by his jubilant mechanics after wining the 1957 British Grand Prix. The Vanwall had scored the first British grande epreuve win for 33 years.

Vanwall

1958 Vanwall

The 2½-litre Vanwall was the fastest car on the grand prix circuits in 1958 and secured the Constructors' Championship for team owner Tony Vandervell, though the team no.1 driver, Stirling Moss failed to win the Drivers' Championship by the narrowest margin of one point.

Vanwall

The 1957/58 Vanwall engine.

Moss in the 1958 Monaco Grand Prix. The nose of the Vanwall was shortened to reduce the possibility of accidental damage.

already retired. Using the straight-line speed of the Vanwall, Schell caught up with the Lancia-Ferrari trio leading the race, got in amongst them and ran as high as second before injector-pump problems dropped him back. That was the high point of 1956. For the rest of the season it was a story of retirements, but Silverstone and Reims had shown that the Vanwall was now a car to be reckoned with.

The de Dion rear suspension was revised for 1957 and more power was found from the engine. For Tony Vandervell, best of all, he finally secured the services of Moss for the season and Tony Brooks was also signed up. The first outing was at Syracuse where Moss, having led, dropped back with a broken injector pipe. Once going again he came up to third. At Monaco, Moss led until he crashed, then Brooks came up to finish second behind Fangio's Maserati.

New drivers had to be found for the French G.P. at Rouen as Moss had injured himself water-skiing and Brooks was suffering from burns he received at Le Mans. Stuart Lewis-Evans, who had been most successful with a 500 cc Cooper, and Roy Salvadori took over. Both retired with minor bothers but had another chance in the G.P. at Reims, where Lewis-Evans led for half the race until he dropped to third with an oil leak.

Moss and Brooks were back for the British G.P. at Aintree, joined by Lewis-Evans. Moss led for 20 laps but stopped with a misfire and so he took over Brooks's car as Brooks was still not fully fit. Moss stormed through the field from ninth place to take the lead and go on to win. It was a historic victory and the first by a British car in a *grande epreuve* for 33 years. It was also a fitting reward for all the resources which Tony Vandervell had put into Vanwall, whose cars were built to exquisite tool-room standards.

There was a setback in the German G.P, the 'Ring and the Vanwall suspension not being compatible. The Pescara G.P. in Italy had been promoted to a World Championship event; Moss ran away from the field to score a second Vanwall victory. It had been Vandervell's declared aim 'to beat those bloody red cars'. Following Pescara, his hopes were triumphantly fulfilled when Moss beat the Maserati and Ferrari teams to win the Italian G.P. at Monza. The season's results saw Moss take second place in the World Championship.

The Grand Prix rules changed for the 1958 season. World Championship races were reduced to 200 miles (300 kms) and the cars had to run on aviation petrol. Exotic alcohol-based fuels with nitromethane were no longer allowed. Vanwall continued with Moss, Brooks and Lewis-Evans in its cockpits.

The season began badly as all three cars dropped out of the Monaco G.P., but Moss went on to win the Dutch G.P. although the other two drivers retired. Brooks was victorious at Spa in the Belgian G.P. and Lewis-Evans was third, but Moss went out on the first lap. In the French G.P. at Reims the Ferrari Dino 246 was the faster car, Hawthorn's Dino 246 running away with the race, leaving Moss to settle for second place. It was a tragic race as Hawthorn's team mate Luigi Musso was killed.

In front of the home crowd at Silverstone Vanwall had a bad day. Moss led but dropped out and Collins's Ferrari won. Lewis-Evans was fourth and Brooks seventh. There was more tragedy in the German G.P. when the likeable Collins, who had driven the Thin Wall Special and the first Vanwall, was killed. Moss fell out again after leading the race, but Brooks was the winner. In Portugal Moss was the victor with Lewis-Evans in third place. In the Italian G.P. at Monza, Moss – for whom the World Championship was almost in his grasp – dropped out and Brooks was the winner.

The final round of the Championship was in Morocco, the only time Formula 1 World Championship racing visited North Africa. Moss won but lost the championship by one point to Hawthorn who came second. The race was a tragedy for Vanwall as Lewis-Evans crashed and died later from burns. Vanwall won the newly instituted Constructors' Championship, but the death of Lewis-Evans deeply affected Tony Vandervell. In January 1959 it was announced that Vanwall was withdrawing from racing.

Although there were infrequent entries of a single low-line Vanwall in 1959 and 1960, and an experimental rear-engined car had one outing in 1960, the magnificent story was over. Tony Vandervell died in 1967. His dedication and determination had put Britain on the map in Grand Prix racing. Vanwall started a run of success for British Racing Green which has been maintained ever since.

Tony Brooks on his way to victory in the 1958 German Grand Prix at the Nürburgring.

The Vanwall swansong. A mechanic drives a Vanwall across the Goodwood paddock at the 1960 Easter meeting. The car was outclassed by the later Coopers and Lotuses in the F1 Glover Trophy and Tony Brooks finished in 7th place.

CHAPTER 12

Cooper: From Backyard Specials to World Champions

DURING the 1920s and 1930s Charles Cooper was a mechanic to Kaye Don, then a leading British racing driver for Sunbeam among other marques. Cooper established a small garage business at Surbiton, south-west of London, where he had an agency for Vauxhall and Austin and did general engineering work. Cooper built an Austin Seven-based special for his son John, born in 1923, who drove it on the road although he was not old enough to hold a driving licence.

At the end of World War Two a group of enthusiasts formed the 500 Club to support a new and cheap class of motor racing for cars with 500 cc motorcycle engines. In 1946 John, who had just been released from the RAF, built a 500 using the front suspension units from two Fiat Topolinos to make a car with independent suspension at the front and rear, powering it with a JAP engine. He was helped by a friend Eric Brandon.

This first Cooper appeared at Prescott hill climb in July 1946. There were problems but by the end of the 1946 season the little car, shared by Cooper and Brandon, was becoming competitive in the fast-growing 500 class. A second car was built for Brandon, who won the first race for 500s at Gransden Lodge in July 1947.

Realising that there was a demand for 500s, Charles and John Cooper reworked the design and went into production, making an initial batch of six which were marketed in 1948. The first batch sold immediately so a second batch of six was started. Altogether 24 cars had been built by the end of 1948. Among the first customers was an 18-year-old virtual novice, Stirling Moss.

The majority of 500s were home-built specials which the production Coopers, finished to a high standard, dominated. Moss won at the first Goodwood meeting in September 1948 and the cars swept the board in the 500 race which preceded the British G.P. at Silverstone in October 1948. During the 1948 season John Cooper ran a car with a 1,000 cc JAP engine in sprints and hill climbs.

A slightly improved 500 was offered for sale for the 1949 season at £575 while the twin-cylinder 1,000 cc JAP engine could be fitted for £775. The 500 cc Coopers, subsequently fitted with Norton engines, continued to dominate the class in 1949 and in every season until the late 1950s when the class, by then Formula 3, fell out of favour. Other British marques, such as Kieft and Staride, offered challenges but none toppled Cooper from its pre-eminent position.

The 1,000 cc Cooper was eligible for 2.0-litre Formula 2 races. Generally little was achieved as the cars were unreliable, but in July 1949 Moss ran his car in the Circuit of Garda in Italy. He came third overall against the 2.0-litre Ferraris and Maseratis, shocking the locals who had ridiculed his bug-like car. Using an 1,100 cc JAP engine, Harry Schell drove the first Cooper in a F1 World Championship event at Monaco in 1950, but was eliminated in a multiple crash on the second lap.

A front-engined Cooper sports car had been built in small numbers using a lengthened chassis with a 1,250 cc MG engine. From this a front-engined F2 car was developed for the 1952 season, fitted with a 1,971 cc Bristol engine. The T20 Cooper-Bristol was simple and light. When the 2.0-litre F2 became the World Championship class, Coopers found themselves in the front line of racing.

The Cooper-Bristols were not fast enough to challenge the Ferraris or Maseratis but had the performance to match the rest. Mike Hawthorn, who had moved up from his Rileys in club racing, was the dominant driver, winning minor races and picking up a number of places through the 1952 season and ending with fifth in the Championship. His performances secured him a place in the Ferrari team in 1953.

The Coopers offered less challenge in 1953, but Moss built a special car designed by Ray Martin and fitted with an Alta engine. Though this was a total failure a second

car, using a standard Cooper chassis, was fast although unreliable. Moss shook the Italian teams with its speed in the Italian G.P. at Monza.

Eric Brandon in the first 500 cc Cooper at Prescott in 1946.

Bill Whitehouse in a Cooper-JAP Mk 4 at Brands Hatch in 1950.

Mike Hawthorn on the start line in his Cooper–Bristol Mk 1 at the 1952 Silverstone International Trophy.

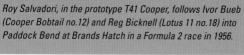

Roy Salvadori, in the prototype T41 Cooper, follows Ivor Bueb (Cooper Bobtail no.12) and Reg Bicknell (Lotus 11 no.18) into Paddock Bend at Brands Hatch in a Formula 2 race in 1956.

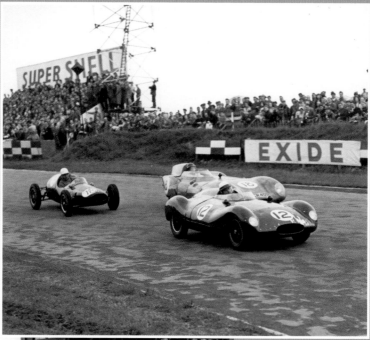

Salvadori (Cooper T43 no.28), Jack Brabham (Cooper T51 no.23) and Chris Bristow (Cooper T51 no.22) share the front row of the grid for the F2 John Davy Trophy at Brands Hatch in 1959.

1960 COOPER TYPE 53

THE 2½-LITRE COVENTRY CLIMAX-ENGINED T53 COOPER DOMINATED THE 1960 GRAND PRIX SEASON. TEAM LEADER, JACK BRABHAM, WON HIS SECOND CHAMPIONSHIP WHILE HIS No.2, BRUCE McLAREN, WAS CHAMPIONSHIP RUNNER-UP. THEIR SUCCESSES SECURED THE CONSTRUCTORS' CHAMPIONSHIP FOR COOPER, BUT AFTER THAT COOPER BEGAN TO FADE AWAY.

Jack Brabham in his 'low-line' T53 Cooper-Climax which took him to the 1960 World Championship.

Bruce McLaren on the grid in the T77 Cooper-Climax V-8 (no.9) at the 1965 United States Grand Prix.

The 2½-litre F1 formula began in 1954 and Cooper, lacking a suitable engine, marked time. Meanwhile a special chassis was built and fitted with a Jaguar engine, creating the sports-racing T33 Cooper-Jaguar. In 1955 a 1,100 cc Coventry-Climax engine was fitted into the rear of an evolved 500 cc chassis and given enclosed bodywork with a central driving seat. This was the famous T39 'Bobtail' sports-racing car which fought with Lotus for supremacy in the 1,100 cc and 1,500 cc classes during the next two seasons.

Early in 1955 an Australian driver, Jack Brabham, who had raced a Cooper-Bristol in Australia, appeared at Surbiton and began working as a mechanic and general helper. Brabham built up a 'Bobtail' with a 2.0-litre Bristol engine and ran this in the 1955 British G.P. at Aintree. It retired, but at the end of the season had a wheel-to-wheel battle with Moss's 250 F Maserati in a minor race at Snetterton. Although not appreciated at the time, this race was a significant event in motor racing history.

When the FIA announced that a new F2 for 1,500 cc unblown cars would begin in 1957, Cooper was quickly off the mark, producing a prototype, the T41, which was virtually an open-wheel 'Bobtail' using a single-cam Coventry Climax engine. Running in a handful of races for the new formula which were put on by British promoters in 1956, this swept the board.

When the formula proper began in 1957, Cooper was ready with the T43. Coventry-Climax produced the FPF, a new twin-cam engine. FPF-powered Coopers dominated F2 races and also appeared in F1 World Championship events. With only 1,500 cc the cars were not fast enough to challenge for the lead, but nabbed some minor places.

Among those who fielded Coopers was Rob Walker, the Johnnie Walker whisky heir, who had raced before World War Two. Latterly he had been one of the most active private entrants in F1 and F2. His F2 Cooper had been successful in 1957, driven by Tony Brooks. This car, a T43 with a 1.9-litre engine, was driven by Moss in the Argentine G.P., the first Championship round in 1958. The regular teams were aghast as Moss won, defeating Ferrari's latest Dino 246 F1.

The T81 Cooper-Maserati entered by Rob Walker for Jo Siffert at the 1966 Silverstone International Trophy.

To show that it was not a fluke, Walker's new T45 was then driven to victory at Monaco by Maurice Trintignant. In a works T45, with a 2.2-litre engine, Salvadori was third in the German G.P, so Cooper finished 1958 in third place in the Constructors' Championship. In F2 Ferrari and Porsche had entered the lists, but Coopers still won most of the races. A young New Zealander, Bruce McLaren, joined the Cooper team and showed great promise.

In 1959 the whole face of motor racing changed. The front-engined GP cars were obsolete and the rear-engined contrivances ruled the roost. Cooper produced an improved T51 for the works team and for sale to customers. With the withdrawal of Vanwall, Moss, ever relishing the role of underdog, elected not to sign with a works team and joined forces with Walker, whose team became a full F1 front runner.

The FPF engine was enlarged to a full 2½ litres. Cooper had built a gearbox for the works cars to cope with the extra power, but this was not available for the Walker team, who used a box designed and built by the Italian specialist, Valerio Colotti. Jack Brabham, who had been improving rapidly as a works driver in F1 and F2, now became the Cooper number one driver and was joined by McLaren, as Salvadori had departed to drive the new F1 Aston Martin.

The 1959 season became a three-cornered battle for the Championship among Moss, Brabham and Tony Brooks, driving for Ferrari. Moss was let down by the Colotti gearbox whose machining faults cost him several races and the Championship. He drove a BRM while the gearbox was revised and ended the season winning with his Cooper-Climax in Portugal and at Monza. Brabham was the World Champion. Although he only won at Monaco and Aintree, he picked up one second and two third places whereas Moss either won or retired. The combined results of Moss and Brabham, together with a

SIR JACK BRABHAM
Sir Jack Brabham was born in Sydney in 1926 and served in the RAAF during the Second World War as a Flight Mechanic. After gaining the Australian midget-car and hill climb championships he came to England in 1955 and worked for Cooper as a mechanic. He built the first rear-engined F1 Cooper, which he drove in the 1955 British G.P.

John Cooper recognised Brabham's remarkable talents as a driver and development engineer, making him a regular works driver in 1956. In 1957 he spent much time developing the F2 Cooper which grew into a full F1 car in 1958. In 1959, as Cooper's number one driver, he took the World Championship with two wins and consistent placings. He did it again more convincingly in 1960, scoring five wins.

Frustrated with the conservative approach of the Coopers, Jack Brabham broke away in 1962 to become a manufacturer. He built F2, F3 and sports cars for sale in a small works at Byfleet, south-west of London, while continuing to drive in F1 himself.

After four development seasons it all came good with the new 3.0-litre Formula 1 in 1966. Brabham worked closely with the Australian engineering company Repco to create a V-8 engine using a GM stock block. This took him to the 1966 Championship, making him the only driver ever to be World Champion in a car bearing his own name. He also took the Constructors' title. Jack Brabham was the Constructors' champion again in 1967 and runner-up in the World Championship behind his team-mate Denny Hulme.

The Repco-Brabhams were outclassed in 1968. Brabham carried on in 1969 using the DFV Ford-Cosworth engine. He intended to retire at the end of 1969 but problems in finding drivers forced him to carry on in 1970. He scored his last win in South Africa. Indeed he might have been Champion again but for two last-lap failures while in the lead.

At the end of 1970 Brabham retired from the sport, selling his interest in the Brabham company to Ron Tauranac, a fellow Australian who had worked with him in building it up. Brabham continues to keep strong connections with motor racing. His sons Geoff, Gary, and David have all become successful drivers. The no-nonsense Australian's exploits were recognised when he was knighted in 1979.

John Cooper after his investiture as a CBE in 2000.

Climax-powered. Cooper replied with Owen Maddock's design for a lower, sleeker car, the T53, which took Brabham to his second World Championship. He won the Dutch, Belgian, French, British and Portuguese G.Ps. His dominance was aided by the absence of Moss, who was out of action for a large part of the season after his Lotus 18 crashed at Spa following a suspension failure. McLaren was the ideal team number two, following Brabham home in several races as well as winning in Argentina, and took second place in the Championship. These successes maintained Cooper dominance in the Constructors' Championship for the second year.

Such are the twists of fate that motor racing offers to its devotees that the dominance of Cooper was over, though it was not evident at that time. A fault of the Cooper set-up was that Charles Cooper became resentful of the efforts of his drivers to improve the cars. This was to lead first Jack Brabham and later Bruce McLaren to leave the team in frustration, both drivers with insight and know-how that allowed them to start their own successful teams.

When F1 changed to 1½-litre unsupercharged cars in 1961, in company with the other British teams Cooper was unready as it was waiting for the promised V-8 Climax. The FPF unit was unable to match the power of the Ferrari and there was little to show in 1961. The prototype V-8 Climax was fitted to Brabham's car for three races but had teething problems with its cooling system. After a dismal season the best that Cooper could show was two fourth places and fourth place among the constructors.

At the end of 1961 Brabham left Cooper to start his own marque, but during that year he and Cooper had opened a small window into an arena where British cars would soon become a powerful force. A modified T53, fitted with a 2.7-litre FPF engine, went to the Indianapolis 500 where despite the lack of power compared to the 4.2-litre Indy cars, Brabham finished ninth.

Much of Cooper's success in F1 had been owed to Brabham who was that remarkable combination of top-class driver and highly competent engineer. The motor racing world was changing with the scientific approach to racing car design, which grew into the billion-pound technological world of the 21st century, starting to emerge. The garage workshop skills which had served Cooper so well for over a decade would no longer be adequate.

With his new V-8 Climax-engined T60, McLaren won at Monaco and in the non-Championship race at

dramatic last-minute win for McLaren in the United States G.P, secured the Constructors' Championship for Cooper by a substantial margin.

A strong rival to Cooper appeared in 1960 when Colin Chapman produced his rear-engined Lotus 18, also

Reims, while Tony Maggs, the South African who had taken Brabham's seat, was second in the French G.P. There was little else to show for 1962. Ken Tyrrell, who had raced a Cooper 500 in the 1950s, took over the management of the F1 team in 1963 after John Cooper was badly hurt in a road accident, but it was a lean year. It was the same in 1964 when 1961 World Champion Phil Hill joined McLaren in the team. The best placing was McLaren's second at Monza.

Charles Cooper, who had kept close watch over the company's purse strings from the beginning, died in October 1964, aged 71. The 1965 season saw no improvement in Cooper's fortunes and at the end of the season Bruce McLaren left to start his own venture. F1 returned to power with the introduction of the 3.0-litre formula in 1966. In May of that year John Cooper relinquished control when the Cooper Car Co. was sold to the Chipstead Motor Group.

Chipstead had strong connections with Maserati, so for the new formula V-12 Maserati engines were supplied to Cooper. Although larger and heavier than some of its rivals, rolling on a monocoque chassis designed by Derrick White, the T81 Cooper-Maserati was undeniably powerful. Jochen Rindt and Ritchie Ginther were the drivers for team manager Roy Salvadori but in mid-season John Surtees, who had left Ferrari after a row, joined the team. At the end of the season Surtees gave the team its first success in four years by winning the Mexican G.P.

In 1967, Surtees went to Honda and Rindt was joined by Pedro Rodriguez. The Mexican gave the team high hopes by winning the South African G.P, but that was to be the last Championship victory for Cooper. After that it was a relentless downward progression. The V-12 BRM engine replaced the Maserati in 1968, but Cooper finally withdrew from F1 at the end of that season.

Meanwhile Cooper had flourished in other formulas. The 500 cc class ran out of steam in the late 1950s and was replaced by Formula Junior, which used production 1,000 and 1,100 cc engines; FJ became F3 in 1963. Cooper built FJ and F3 cars and had a deal with BMC to use the Group's engines. The FJ/F3 Coopers helped both John Surtees and Jackie Stewart towards the top in motor racing and gained many successes while never quite dominating.

The remarkable BMC Mini appeared in 1959. John Cooper felt that a tuned version had great possibilities. He developed a prototype and BMC agreed to produce it in 1,071 cc form, called the Mini-Cooper. Appearing toward the end of 1961, it was given a boost when the

British Touring Car Championship was won by Sir John Whitmore in an 850 cc Mini.

The Mini-Cooper, which grew after a season into the more highly-tuned Mini-Cooper S, swept the board in racing and rallies. The British Saloon Car Championship was taken in 1962 and the European Championship was secured in 1964. Championship class wins followed for several years. A final British Championship was won in 1969.

Even bigger victories came in rallying. A Mini-Cooper S won the 1964 Monte Carlo rally driven by Paddy Hopkirk. Timo Makinen repeated this success in 1965, while there was another Monte win by Rauno Aaltonen in 1967. The works Mini-Coopers gained many victories in other rallies until the design was finally overtaken by time. The Mini in its many forms has been the backbone of British club racing and rallying for nearly 50 years.

John Cooper died at Christmas 2000, aged 77. His remarkable work had been recognised 12 months before his death, when he was appointed a Companion of the Order of the British Empire (CBE). The Coopers, father and son, became true production manufacturers of racing cars, building some 1,400 cars in their Surbiton works. Using their practical and often home-spun approach, they made some remarkable and innovative cars which gained huge prestige for Britain.

An early Mini outing. Tony Ambrose and Alec Pitts with an 850 Mini prior to leaving England for the 1960 Monte Carlo Rally.

CHAPTER 13

Jaguar: Lyons – Hearted Racers

WILLIAM LYONS was born in Blackpool in 1901. In 1923, with William Walmsley, he founded the Swallow Sidecar Co. making motorcycle sidecars. In 1926 Swallow expanded and began to make stylish bodies for the Austin Seven. The company prospered, moving nearer the centre of the motor industry in Coventry.

In 1931 a Swallow body was fitted to a Standard chassis to make the SS1 with a 2,054 cc side-valve Standard engine, followed by the SSII with a 1,005 cc engine. These had a strikingly handsome appearance and sold well, so in 1934, SS Cars Ltd was formed. The first competition appearance of an SS was in the 1932 RAC Rally. SS cars made regular appearances in rallies. A team of three cars tackled the 1933 Alpine Trial, but without success. The team returned in 1934 and took the third-place team prize in their class.

A new short-chassis sports car appeared in 1935, the SS90, but this was a stop-gap until a new car, with an overhead-valve cylinder head fitted to the 2½-litre Standard engine, arrived in 1936. This was the SS100 and the cars were now known as SS Jaguars. The SS100, a proper sports car, made its mark immediately by winning a Glacier Cup for a faultless run in the 1936 Alpine Trial.

The first outright racing successes came in 1936 when Casimiro d'Oliviera won a minor sports car race on the Villa Real circuit in Portugal and the Australian driver Freddie McEvoy won the 3.0-litre class of the G.P. de la Marne on the fast Rheims circuit. A 3½-litre version of the SS100 appeared in 1937. Up to the start of World War Two in 1939, the potent and handsome SS100 gained a string of successes in British rallies and in minor races at Brooklands, Donington and Crystal Palace.

William Lyons knew the car was fragile and did not encourage owners to enter long-distance races, but it showed its performance when a stripped works car lapped Brooklands at 118 mph. Mindful of the wartime connotation of 'SS', the company was re-named Jaguar Cars Ltd in 1945.

During the war the ambitious Lyons had supervised and encouraged the design of a twin-overhead-camshaft engine by Walter Heynes, the company's chief engineer, assisted by Harry Mundy and Walter Hassan, who had been a Bentley racing mechanic in the 1920s. This engine, the legendary XK six, went into a new sports car, the XK120, which was announced at the 1948 London Motor Show.

The XK120 made its competition debut in the one-hour production sports car race at the 1949 International

Trophy meeting at Silverstone and swept the board. A full works racing programme began in 1950, gaining a fifth place in the Mille Miglia and a car running third at Le Mans when it retired. At the end of the 1950 season Stirling Moss won the Ulster Tourist Trophy on the demanding Dundrod circuit with a borrowed XK120. This was a big step, both for the Moss career and for Jaguar, which was becoming as serious a player in major motor racing as it was in the high-performance and luxury-car market.

In 1951 a full-blooded sports-racing car was built around XK120 parts, the C-type. Driven by Peter Whitehead and Peter Walker, it won the Le Mans 24-hour race and gave Moss a second Tourist Trophy victory. In 1952 Jaguar was not so successful on the circuits, a bodywork alteration causing the C-types to overheat and drop out at Le Mans. A Scottish team, Ecurie Ecosse, began racing XK120s and then C-types, financed by Edinburgh accountant David Murray. A blue-painted Ecosse car gained its first win in the 1952 Jersey International sports car race.

Jaguars were also gaining much success in rallying. Ian Appleyard, Lyons's son-in-law, was awarded the first Gold Alpine Cup for winning three successive Alpine Cups in the Alpine Trial with an XK120. The Le Mans failure was redeemed in 1953 when C-types took first, second and fourth places, the winning car driven by Tony Rolt and Duncan Hamilton, helped materially by the innovation of disc brakes.

For 1954 Heynes and aerodynamicist Malcolm Sayer designed a new sports-racer, the D-type, which had a monocoque centre section. Although notable for its smooth aerodynamic body, it retained the faithful XK engine. The D-type was beaten by a Ferrari at Le Mans by a mere 40 seconds, but finished 1-2-3 in the Reims 12-hour race.

The whole face of motor racing changed with the disaster at Le Mans in 1955 when 83 spectators were killed. This accident and the subsequent withdrawal of the remaining two Mercedes-Benz cars, over-shadowed the victory for a D-type driven by Mike Hawthorn and Ivor Bueb. The race was also a personal tragedy for

The SS1 tourer driven by the Hon. Brian Lewis in the 1935 Monte Carlo Rally.

Lyons as his son Michael was killed in a road accident driving to the circuit. Hawthorn had won the Sebring 12-hours with a D-type, but the D-type was unable to beat the 300 SLR Mercedes in a straight fight.

For Jaguar, 1956 began on a high note when a Mark VII saloon won the Monte Carlo Rally driven by Ronnie Adams. Le Mans could have been a fiasco when two of the works D-types were eliminated in a crash on the second lap but the day was saved by Ecurie Ecosse whose D-type, driven by Ron Flockhart and Ninian Sanderson, came home as the winner. At the end of 1956 Jaguar announced that it was withdrawing from factory-backed competition. With four Le Mans wins and success in the Monte – events at the pinnacle of prestige and publicity – there was little to prove or more kudos to be gained. The pressing need was to concentrate on production to meet a huge demand for cars.

The Jaguar XK engine, which first saw the light of day in 1948 in the Jaguar XK 120. This engine was the foundation of Jaguar's post-war success both on the road and on the tracks of the world. It is seen here in 3.4-litre dry sump guise as powering the D-type Jaguar. Carburation was by three Weber 45 DC03s which in Le Mans spec. produced in the region of 285 bhp at around 5,750 revs, with a top speed of 160 mph-plus.

John Craig in an SS100 at Goodwood in 1949. He is followed by the 328 BMW of Tony Crook who later became the proprietor of Bristol cars.

The XK120 Jaguar of Ian and Pat Appleyard in the 1953 Alpine Trial.

Tony Rolt in the pits with the winning C-type at Le Mans in 1953.

The C-type Jaguar driven by Stirling Moss and Peter Walker at the pits during the 1953 Tourist Trophy at Dundrod. Lofty England, the team manager is on the left in the white cap and Peter Walker waits to take the wheel. The car staggered to the finish in fourth place with a broken gearbox.

A pair of works D-type Jaguars at the 1955 BRDC International Trophy meeting at Silverstone. Mike Hawthorn drove No.1 in the sports car race and finished fourth after being slowed by a water leak. This D-type, Reg. No. OKV 3, was the third factory car and carried the chassis number XKC 404 with engine number E2006-9.

The D-type Jaguar after its victory at Le Mans in 1955. Mike Hawthorn is on the left of the car, his co-driver Ivor Bueb is on the right with his back to the camera. It is a subdued celebration following the appalling crash which killed 82 spectators. The crash involved the Mercedes-Benz 300 SLR, No.20, driven by Pierre Levegh colliding with the Austin Healey 100 of Lance Macklin on the pits straight. The Mercedes was catapulted into the crowd and burst into flames - Pierre Levegh was also killed, though Lance Macklin had a lucky escape.

MIKE HAWTHORN

Mike Hawthorn has an immortal place in motor racing history as the first Briton to become World Champion. He was born in 1929. Supported by his father Leslie, who raced motorcycles in the 1920s and 1930s, he began driving Rileys in club events in 1951. When in 1952 F2 became the World Championship, the bow-tied Hawthorn, driving an underpowered Cooper-Bristol, rocketed onto the scene with some notable drives.

Hawthorn's efforts secured him a place in the Ferrari team for 1953, when he beat all the recognised top drivers in winning the French G.P. He stayed with Ferrari in 1954 but signed for Vanwall in 1955. This was premature and he returned to Ferrari midway through the season. Mike drove sports cars for Jaguar and won the ill-fated 1955 Le Mans race in a D-type. He moved to BRM in 1956, but had narrow escapes in two crashes following mechanical failures.

It was back to Ferrari in 1957 and 1958 for Hawthorn, who formed a close relationship with his team-mate Peter Collins, 'Mon Ami Mate'. Collins's death in the 1958 German G.P. hit Hawthorn hard, but he had a consistent season with many places, although only one win in the French G.P. His results gave him the World Championship by one point from Moss. Hawthorn did not enjoy his Champion status for long as he was killed in a road accident in January 1959.

1956 Jaguar D-Type

The 3.4-litre D-type Jaguar driven by Mike Hawthorn and Ivor Bueb won the ill-fated 1955 Le Mans 24-hour race. The D-type also won at Le Mans in 1956 and 1957. The Jaguar's good aerodynamics and straight-line speed made it an ideal car for the fast Le Mans circuit.

Duncan Hamilton (3.4-litre Mk 1 no.4) and Paul Frere (Mk 7 no.2) at the 1956 Silverstone International Trophy meeting.

Although given loyal support in America by the equipe of Briggs Cunningham, whose white cars with blue stripes won many national races, Jaguar participation in international racing became sporadic with little success.

The rapid growth in touring-car racing saw Jaguar on top with the 3.4-litre Mark 1 and 3.8-litre Mark 2 saloons. The cars were unbeatable in British events until Ford's Galaxie and Mustang appeared in the mid-1960s. The German driver Peter Nöcker won the 1963 European Touring Car Championship with a 3.8-litre Mark 2. The E-type was announced in 1961 and was raced immediately by many private owners, some with works support, but lacked the power to beat the GT Ferraris even when developed into the Lightweight model.

In 1966 Jaguar merged with the British Motor Corporation and Lyons relinquished control. This was followed two years later by another merger with Leyland to form the ill-fated British Leyland. In the mid-1960s a return to racing was contemplated with a prototype, the XJ-13, which had a four-cam 5.0-litre V-12 engine, but the scheme was shelved. A new and different V-12 was designed to power the production XJ-12 saloon.

BL decided that a return to racing was necessary to boost the Jaguar image and the two-door XJ-12 saloon was chosen. The car was entrusted to Ralph Broad, a

Ecurie Ecosse continued to race, the Scottish cars winning again at Le Mans in 1957 leading a Jaguar 1-2-3-4, but the D-type was becoming obsolete and the XK engine adapted poorly to a change in the international sports car regulations limiting engine size to 3.0 litres.

The XJ-S which won the 1984 European Touring Car Championship for Tom Walkinshaw.

The 1986 XJR-6.

successful tuner, whose Broadspeed prepared a team for the 1976 season with the European Touring Car Championship as the target. With various delays only one race was contested, but there was a full season in 1977, regrettably unsuccessful.

Scottish driver Tom Walkinshaw, who had built up motoring group TWR in 1981, suggested to Jaguar that he should prepare and run a team of XJ-S coupés in the 1982 European Touring Car championship. The TWR XJ-Ss began to put Jaguar back on the racing map with wins at Brno, the Nürburgring, Silverstone and Zolder and finishing as Championship runners-up. The TWR team was back in 1983 and scored five wins to be runners-up again. They made a renewed effort in 1984. At the third attempt there was real triumph, with four wins including the Spa 24-hours. The XJ-S was the champion car and Walkinshaw the champion driver.

In the USA the V-12 E-type had been prepared and raced with success by Bob Tullius. The successes continued with the XJ-S, resulting in class wins in the TransAm Championship for 1977 and 1978. Group 44, the company founded by Tullius, now received support from Jaguar in the building of a mid-engined sports-racer, the XJR-5, to contest the US-wide IMSA Camel race series in 1982. The car was designed by Lee Dykstra in the Group 44 workshops at Winchester, Virginia.

In 1982 the team was learning, but in 1983 the car won four IMSA rounds and was placed second in the championship. Despite high hopes for 1984 there was only a single IMSA win, although two XJR-5s ran at Le Mans where Tullius led the race for a few laps, but both cars retired. For 1985 TWR was contracted by Jaguar to build a new car, the XJR-6 based on the XJR-5 design, but it was unready for Le Mans and so the XJR-5s came out again and one finished 14th.

Ready at the end of the 1985 season, the XJR-6 came second at Selangor in the final round of the World Endurance Championship. The XJR-6 was raced throughout 1986 in the World Sports Prototype Championship and scored one victory in the Tourist

Trophy at Silverstone while picking up several places during the season.

A new car, the XJR-8, which used carbon fibre in the chassis, was designed by Tony Southgate for TWR's 1987 season, powered by a Jaguar V-12 engine enlarged to 7.0 litres. The season began with excellent wins at Jarama, Jerez, Monza and Silverstone. Failure at Le Mans was followed by wins at Brands Hatch, Nürburgring, Spa and Fuji, so the season ended with the XJR-8 as the World Sports Prototype Champion.

Southgate went back to his drawing board for 1988 and produced the XJR-9, intended for IMSA and the Sports Prototype Championships but with minor differences. The season was a fight between the Jaguar and the turbocharged Sauber-Mercedes. Jaguar began with a win in the Daytona 24-hours and followed with victory at Jarama, Monza and Silverstone, but Sauber won at Jerez and Le Mans was expected to be a fierce battle. After the Saubers were withdrawn with tyre problems the race turned into a struggle between the five Jaguars and a horde of Porsches. The lead changed continuously and at the end the XJR-9 of Jan Lammers, Johnny Dumfries and Andy Wallace was triumphant. The Jaguar went on to win at Brands Hatch and Fuji, securing the World Championship.

The regulations changed for 1989, causing problems as the XJR-9 needed substantial alterations, while TWR was also developing a 3.6-litre turbo V-6 in parallel. The TWR cars picked up some places but there were no wins and the Saubers dominated the season. The V-12 engine went into a new XJR-12 for 1990 which won the Daytona 24-hours, while the Ross Brawn-designed XJR-11 with the V-6 engine ran at Silverstone and won. The XJR-12 came out again for Le Mans. Driven by John Nielsen, Price Cobb and Martin Brundle, it won, while another XJR-12 was third.

The rules changed again for 1991. Brawn designed a new car, the XJR-14, for Walkinshaw which was virtually a two-seat F1 machine. Ford, who now owned Jaguar, decided that it should have a Cosworth HB V-8 engine. While it took first place at Monza, Silverstone and the Nürburgring, the proven XJR-12 came out for Le Mans, taking second, third and fourth places behind a Mazda. Jaguar took the Sports Car World Championship, but it was almost the end of the road. For 1992 the company's efforts went into IMSA and after a few appearances of the XJR-12 in 1993, Jaguar's sports-racing exploits finished.

Ford wanted to enhance Jaguar's image with a return to racing, so in 1999 the Stewart F1 team was purchased. This had been formed by triple World Champion Jackie Stewart in 1997 with Ford support, using a Ford Zetec-R V-10 engine built by Cosworth. It had struggled and had gained only one win, the 1999 European G.P, before Ford bought the team at the end of the 1999 season.

Freshly baptised as Jaguar, the green-painted cars, backed by the huge resources of Ford, were expected to be winners. The results were pitiful. Five seasons brought no wins and only two podium finishes. Ford considered that the outlay had not been justified by the results and the team was sold to the soft drinks company, Red Bull, at the end of 2004.

That was the last appearance of the Jaguar name in top-line motor racing. It had been a long journey from the sidecars in Blackpool, but the seven wins with green cars at Le Mans will ensure that the name is never forgotten.

The XJR-12 on its way to 2nd place at Le Mans in 1991.

F1 disappointment. The Jaguar R1 of 2000.

CHAPTER 14

Lotus: The Appliance of Science

ONE man was the driving force behind Lotus: Colin Chapman. His first Lotus was an Austin Seven special that he built for off-road trials while a student at London University in 1948. The second was a dual-purpose trials and sports-racing car which gained success in club events in 1950.

Chapman became noticed with his Lotus Mk 3, a special built to the 750 formula, created to provide cheap racing using Austin Seven components. With the Mk 3 Chapman brought an innovative approach to the 750 formula, which he dominated in 1951. The first production Lotus, the Mk 6, followed in 1952. Based on Ford 10 components, it found a ready market.

Lotus was growing quickly, although housed in little more than lock-up garages behind a pub belonging to Chapman's father-in-law at Hornsey in North London. The Mk 8 in 1954 moved Chapman and his cars into prominence in international racing. This had a 1,500 cc MG engine in an advanced space-frame chassis with a sleek state-of-the-art body designed by aerodynamicist, Frank Costin. When Chapman beat a works Porsche in a race at Silverstone the world began to take notice to such an extent that he was asked to advise on the chassis development of the GP Vanwall.

In 1955 the Mk 9 was the first Lotus to use the Coventry Climax engine. The major breakthrough came with the Mk 11 in 1956. This sports-racing car was produced in various forms from an 1,172 cc Ford-engined model for competitors in minor club races up to the 1.1- and 1.5-litre Coventry Climax engine for the more serious classes. Before Cooper's rear-engined 'Bobtail' appeared, the Mk 11 dominated the small-capacity classes in national and international events and secured class wins and the Index of Performance at Le Mans.

The moustachioed Chapman had greater ambitions. The first single-seat Lotus, the 12, appeared in 1957 for the newly instituted 1,500 cc Formula 2. The spidery-looking 12 was not especially successful in F2, but at the beginning of 1958 a 2.0-litre FPF Climax engine was fitted and the 12 became the first F1 Lotus. In May 1958 it made its debut in the Aintree 200, driven by Graham Hill, and surprised the racing world by finishing fourth in the Belgian G.P. in the hands of Cliff Allison.

For the 1958 French G.P. a new car, the 16, was produced. This was a much more advanced design with an offset engine canted on its side and with Lotus's own transmission. In appearance the 16 was a miniature Vanwall, but it was a disappointment, plagued with many problems, gaining negligible results in 1958 and 1959.

At the 1957 London Motor Show the Lotus Elite was unveiled. All previous Lotuses, including the Mk 6, had been designed as competition cars, but the Elite, which had a Climax engine, was intended to be a road car as well. Breaking new ground as a glass-fibre monocoque coupé, the Elite is considered by many to be one of the most beautiful cars ever made.

As a road car the Elite was less than successful, the monocoque giving problems and it was noisy, but in competition it was almost unbeatable in the small GT class and gained several international wins. The introduction of the Elite saw Lotus move from its first small workshops in North London to a new factory at Cheshunt in Hertfordshire.

While Colin Chapman is widely regarded as a prime technical innovator, it would probably be more accurate to say that he had a great flair in identifying the innovations of others and then using and exploiting those ideas which would work successfully. From his early days he surrounded himself with competent engineers and designers. Thus many ideas and innovations credited to Chapman actually came from those who worked with him, who were fired by his enthusiasm and single-minded dedication.

The big breakthrough in racing came in 1960 with the Lotus 18. This, the first rear-engined Lotus, was a relatively simple design which was used for F1, F2 and the newly introduced Formula Junior. The 18 was an instant success. After winning some minor races it gained the first Lotus World Championship win when Stirling Moss was victorious at Monaco in an 18 owned by Rob Walker. Unfortunately a Lotus flaw was the culprit when Moss crashed at Spa in practice after the suspension of his 18 failed and he was badly hurt. The works Lotus drivers lacked the pace of Brabham's Cooper which dominated the season until Moss returned and took the United States G.P. at the end of 1960, the final race of the 2½-litre Formula 1.

When the 1,500 cc GP formula began in 1961 it was a difficult year for Lotus, which lacked a suitable engine, in company with the other British teams. Nevertheless Moss gained remarkable wins in the Monaco and German G.Ps with an 18, his driving and its handling overmatching the power of the Ferraris which dominated the rest of the season's Championship races.

Jim Clark, a new Scottish driver who had been supreme in FJ with an 18 in 1960, joined the Lotus F1 team. In company with the other British manufacturers, Lotus received the V-8 Coventry Climax engine for the 1962 season. Initially it was used in the tube-framed 24

but a new car, the 25, was designed with a 'monocoque' chassis comprising two fabricated bays carrying the fuel tanks. With it, Jim Clark gained wins in the Belgian, British and United States G.Ps. The ultra-slim Lotus 25 was to influence a generation of racing car builders.

The Elite was replaced by the Elan in 1962. This had a Lotus twin-cam head on a Ford engine and, like the Elite, was a very successful GT racer. The Lotus twin-cam engine also went into a very rapid sports-racer, the 23, which was excluded by the Le Mans scrutineers on flimsy grounds as it posed a major menace to the French cars in its class. In 1963 Clark and the Lotus 25 were pre-eminent, winning seven of the ten World Championship races and taking the crown. Reliability problems kept Clark from sweeping the board in 1964, though he won three Championship rounds.

Meanwhile Lotus was building a close relationship with Ford. Its twin-cam head went onto the Ford Cortina engine to create the Lotus Cortina which became a formidable racing and rally saloon car, winning the British Touring Car Championship in 1963 and 1964. More significant was the collaboration which produced the Lotus 29. This had a race-tuned 4.2-litre Ford Fairlane

Peter Gammon's MG-engined Lotus 6 dominated its class in British events in 1954.

The Lotus 12; the first single-seater is shown at the 1956 London Motor Show.

V-8 that took Clark to second place in the Indianapolis 500 in 1963. He dropped out of the 1964 '500' when in the lead but came back in 1965 to win the race in a Lotus 38, the first British car to gain victory at the Brickyard, a win which ranks in significance with the Sunbeam victory at Tours in 1923.

The 1965 season also saw Clark dominating the World Championship again in a Lotus 33, a development of the 25, winning six of the ten rounds. Not all Lotus efforts were crowned with success, however. A 4.2-litre Ford-engined sports-racer, the 30, was a failure and a development, the 40, was described as 'a 30 with ten more faults'.

In 1966 Lotus marked time while waiting for a suitable engine for the new 3.0-litre GP formula. An H-16 BRM engine gave Clark a win in the United States G.P. Meanwhile Ford was financing the development of the Cosworth DFV V-8, the greatest engine ever to appear in G.P. racing. Lotus had the exclusive use of this when it arrived in 1967. The DFV was fitted to a new car, the

Cliff Allison in a Lotus 11 at the 1956 Silverstone International Trophy meeting.

49, whose first race was the Dutch G.P. Clark left the rest of the field struggling in his wake. Neither car nor engine was wholly reliable but he went on to win the British, US and Mexican G.Ps.

After commercial advertising was permitted on F1 cars in 1968, Lotus was one of the first to sign up with a sponsor, the tobacco company, Gold Leaf. Thus the familiar green with a yellow stripe was replaced with a red, gold and white livery. Clark began the season with a win in the South African G.P. but the whole motor racing world was shattered when he was killed in April, driving an F2 Lotus at Hockenheim. His death was a huge blow not only to Chapman personally and to the Lotus team but also to the world of racing.

Graham Hill, who had rejoined Lotus at the beginning of 1967, took over the number one seat and did a fine job, winning in Spain, Monaco and Mexico to take the World Championship and the Constructors' title for Lotus. Lotus returned to Indianapolis in 1968, with the Type 56 which had a Pratt & Whitney gas turbine, but it crashed in practice and the driver, Mike Spence, was killed, an additional blow to the team so soon after Clark's death.

Jochen Rindt joined Hill in 1969, but the going was harder now that the DFV had been supplied to other teams and the advantage it had given Lotus had gone. Wins at Monaco, Mexico and the United States were all that could be achieved. Hill left the team after a serious accident in the US G.P.

For 1970 Chapman had hoped to gain an advantage with four-wheel drive, but abandoned it as unpromising. A new car, the 72, appeared. The work of Maurice Philippe, this was one of the first F1 cars to exploit

The Lotus Elite of the French drivers, Vidilles and Malle, which retired at Le Mans in 1959.

Stirling Moss beat the more powerful Ferraris with his Lotus 18 at Monaco in 1961.

The Lotus 25 at its debut, the 1962 Dutch Grand Prix.

Jim Clark on his way to victory in the 1965 Indianapolis 500 with the Lotus-Ford 38

Art Pollard with the Pratt & Whitney turbine-powered Lotus 56 in the 1968 Indianapolis 500. He retired after 168 laps with a broken fuel pump drive.

The Constructors' crown was also secured in 1973. The 72 was still the best car in the field and Fittipaldi won three Championship rounds, while his new team-mate, the Swedish driver Ronnie Peterson, won four, but the Championship went to Jackie Stewart in a Tyrrell. In 1974 Fittipaldi had gone to McLaren and Peterson was the number one driver for Lotus, but the 72 was becoming dated.

In 1968 Lotus had become a public company with a new factory at Hethel in Norfolk. Chapman had hived off Team Lotus and the racing activities as a separate organisation. Peterson won the Monaco, French and Italian G.Ps but it was a struggle and a new car, the Type 76, was a failure.

aerodynamic downforce with its wedge profile. With it Rindt won the Monaco, Dutch, French, British and German G.Ps. This secured him the World Championship, but it was a posthumous title as he was killed in practice for the Italian G.P. at Monza. His place in the Lotus team was taken at the end of the season by a brilliant newcomer, Brazilian Emerson Fittipaldi, who had been unbeatable in F3. He won the US G.P, the last race of the season, giving Lotus a bitter-sweet Constructors' title and securing a posthumous Drivers' title for Rindt.

During 1970, there had been experiments with a gas-turbine F1 car, following up on the wedge-shaped cars raced at Indy, but the project was abandoned. The year 1971 was poor for Lotus with little to show, but the team, now with John Player sponsorship, came back with a bang in 1972. Now in black and gold, the cars had five wins in Championship rounds. Fittipaldi was Champion and Lotus had the Constructors' title.

The struggle continued through 1975 with the outclassed 72 gaining minimal results. A new car, the 77, came out for 1976, but it had problems and Peterson left the team and was replaced by American ace, Mario Andretti. Tony Southgate had joined Lotus as chief designer and made some revisions to the 77 which helped Andretti to win the Japan G.P. at the end of the season.

Massive research had been done at Lotus on aerodynamics, ground effects and downforce, led by Peter Wright. The result was the Type 78 which came out for the 1977 season. This gave Andretti wins in the US (West), Spanish, French and Italian G.Ps and so he took third place in the World Championship and Lotus were runners-up among the constructors.

Prospects were even better in 1978, Lotus's rivals not yet having figured out how downforce was generated. The team started the year with the 78 but in mid-season the Type 79, a redesign with all the experience learned from the 78, appeared and extended the Lotus dominance.

Ronnie Peterson in the 1974 Lotus 72. The front wing has been 'nudged'.

1967 Lotus 49

The Lotus 49 with the DFV Cosworth engine won its first race, the 1967 Dutch Grand Prix, driven by Jim Clark. This was the first of 155 grand prix wins for the Cosworth-Ford engine. It was also the last season in which grand prix cars raced in national colours. Commercial sponsors' colours have predominated since then.

JIM CLARK

Jim Clark was perhaps the only British driver who rivalled the successful versatility of Stirling Moss. Born in Fifeshire, Scotland in 1936, Clark began driving a Porsche in club races in 1958. In 1960 he joined the Lotus Formula Junior works team, dominating the class to such an extent that he had moved up the F1 Team Lotus by mid-season.

The 1961 season was thin for Lotus, in common with the other British F1 teams, as it waited for the V-8 Climax engine, but in 1962 Clark won his first World Championship race in Belgium and followed this with two more wins to become runner-up in the Championship.

In 1963 Clark and the Lotus 25 were an unbeatable combination. With seven wins he dominated the Championship. Meanwhile he was driving for Lotus in sports car races and gaining many successes with a Lotus-Cortina in saloon car events. As further evidence of his versatility he took third place in the Indy 500 with a Lotus-Ford.

An oil leak in the last round in Mexico cost Clark the 1964 Championship by one point, despite six wins, but in 1965 it was Clark again. Six wins secured the World Championship and there was lucrative triumph at Indianapolis.

The new 3.0-litre F1 saw Lotus waiting for the DFV Ford-Cosworth engine and so 1966 was a lean year for Clark too, though he eked out a BRM-powered win at Watkins Glen. With the DFV in the Lotus 49 he was back on form in 1967, but he either won or dropped out and so did not secure the Championship.

Auguries were good for 1968 with a win in the first F1 round in South Africa. Then Clark drove an F2 Lotus at Hockenheim in Germany. Victim of a slow puncture, he went off the road, hit a tree and was killed instantly. The motor racing world was shattered by the death of the seemingly untouchable Jim Clark.

Jim Clark tests the Lotus-Ford 38 at Snetterton before its foray to the Indianapolis 'Brickyard' where it won the 1965 500-Miles.

Andretti had six wins, while Peterson – who had returned to Lotus – scored two. Then it went sadly wrong. In a first-lap accident in the Italian G.P. at Monza, Peterson crashed and later died from his injuries. The season's results gave Andretti and Peterson first and second places in the World Championship while Lotus swept away with the Constructors' title.

Martini replaced John Player as the sponsors in 1979 and so the cars were painted green again, now with an olive tinge. Another improved design, the Type 80, came out but it was a step too far, suffering many problems. The 79 had been caught by the opposition – especially by a superior copy by Williams – so there was little to show. It was the same story in 1980. Essex, a fuel company, had become the main sponsor, but the 81, to some extent a re-worked 79, was not up to the task.

For 1981 a revolutionary design, the Type 88, was produced. This had a so-called 'twin chassis' to exploit the benefits of downforce and made extensive use of carbon fibre, but the design was banned by the FISA and a conventional Type 87 was used instead. John Player sponsorship replaced Essex during the season, but the results were dismal again. Elio de Angelis and Nigel Mansell were the drivers for 1982. Using a Type 91, a cleaned-up 87, de Angelis won the Austrian G.P., scoring the 150th victory for the Cosworth DFV engine.

Lotus received a blow from which its racing activities never fully recovered when Colin Chapman died from a heart attack in December 1982. Had he survived, his personal future might have been problematic as there were suggestions he was involved in the financial scandals surrounding the design work undertaken by Lotus on the DeLorean project.

Despite Chapman's death, Team Lotus carried on. In 1983 the French designer, Gerard Ducarouge, was employed. He came up with a new series of cars using a V-6 1,500 cc Renault turbo-blown engine. The Type 94/98Ts raced from 1983 until 1986. De Angelis and Mansell scored no wins but gained several places. In 1985 Ayrton Senna was signed. The brilliance of the Brazilian was evident immediately as he won in Portugal in his second race and also won the Belgian G.P. at Spa. It was an erratic season as he was either placed or the car failed.

It was the same story in 1986 with wins in Spain and the United States – and many failures. For 1987 Lotus used a V-6 Honda engine in the 99T and found sponsorship from Camel cigarettes. Senna picked up wins at Monaco and in the United States, but at the end of the season he moved on to McLaren where he took the 1988 Championship. Lotus signed up Nelson Piquet, the 1987 Champion, but despite his undoubted skill, 1988 was a poor season. In 1989 the Honda support was lost and Lotus had to rely on the British Judd CV V-8 engine. Its fortunes continued to deteriorate and its new 101 was among the back markers.

The end of the road was nearing for the once-great Lotus in F1. Lamborghini engines were tried in 1990. Between 1991 and 1995 there were reorganisations. The Cosworth-Ford HB V-8 and Mugen-Honda V-10 were used and drivers of the quality of Mika Häkkinen and Johnny Herbert were signed up, but the results did not come.

Lotus finally faded away after an amalgamation in 1995 with the Pacific F1 team, which soon disappeared. In its great years Team Lotus had been magnificent. It was sad that a marque which had won 79 F1 World Championship races and seven Constructors' Championships ended in such mediocrity.

Ronnie Peterson trying hard with the Lotus 79 in the 1978 Dutch Grand Prix.

CHAPTER 15

Brabham: Dual Champion

ALTHOUGH Jack Brabham had been World Champion in 1959 and 1960 driving Coopers, he was frustrated by that little company's reluctance to take risks to advance its designs. He felt that the somewhat basic Cooper designs could be bettered. Discreetly he joined forces with Ron Tauranac, an engineer with whom he had worked closely in his early racing years in Australia. Tauranac had designed a Formula Junior, the MRD, which was the first prototype Brabham. It raced with some success in 1961.

In 1962 Brabham left Cooper and raced a Lotus 24 with a V-8 Climax engine in F1, while the MRD went into series production as a 'Brabham' in a small workshop in Surbiton near the Cooper works. The FJ Brabham became the dominant car in the class, 33 being built by the end of 1963. The first F1 Brabham, the BT3 with a V-8 Climax engine, appeared at the 1962 German GP, driven by the boss himself. Brabham ran it for the rest of the season and picked up some minor places before coming second in the non-Championship Mexican GP.

In 1963 Brabham was joined by the American driver, Dan Gurney, then at the peak of his considerable powers, but it was the year when Jim Clark was dominant and the BT7 Brabhams picked up only minor places. Brabham did win the Australian GP with a 2.7-litre Climax-engined

car and also won two non-Championship F1 races. The BT7 had been developed into the BT11, with which Gurney scored the first Championship wins for the marque, winning the French and Mexican GPs in 1964.

In a new 1.0-litre F2, instituted in 1964, Brabham scored several wins in an SCA Cosworth-engined car. Another lean year came in 1965; Brabham and Gurney picked up places but there was no win. For some races they were joined by New Zealander Denny Hulme, who had been highly successful in an FJ Brabham. The company had moved to a factory at Weybridge, near Brooklands, where in 1964 and 1965 it made a sports-racing car, the BT8, with an FPF Climax engine. Of the 14 built, Hulme used one to win the 1965 Tourist Trophy at Oulton Park.

When the Grand Prix formula changed to 3.0 litres unsupercharged in 1966 Brabham, unlike the other British teams, was ready. From his early days he had worked closely with the Australian engineering company, Repco, which had given him engineering and financial assistance and had played an important part in setting up MRD to manufacture Brabhams. Following Brabham's instructions and to designs by Phil Irving, Repco's engineers produced a V-8 engine based on a stock GM aluminium cylinder block fitted with single-overhead-camshaft heads.

This light and simple unit went into a new BT20. With this Brabham won the French, Dutch, British and German GPs to take the World Championship, the only driver ever to do so in a car of his own manufacture. Missing a great opportunity, Gurney had departed to race his own F1 Eagle, so Hulme was picked to back up Brabham, helping the marque to win the Constructors' Championship.

For the 1967 season the rival teams had their new engines, all developing more power than the Repco unit, but good driving and reliability secured the World Championship for Hulme, who won the Monaco and German GPs and picked several second places, while Brabham was the runner-up with wins in the French and Canadian GPs. This secured the Constructors' title for Brabham for the second year.

The Austrian, Jochen Rindt, a regular winner in F2 during 1967 with a Brabham BT 23, joined the F1 team for 1968 as Hulme had gone to join fellow Kiwi, McLaren. Looking for more power, twin-cam heads were fitted to the Repco engine, installed in a new BT26. Although the car was quick it was unreliable and the results were disappointing and Brabham and Rindt had little to show at the end of the season.

With no development potential left in the Repco, for 1969 Brabham joined the rest and fitted the DFV Cosworth engine into the BT26 which, unlike the other British F1 cars, still relied on a space frame. Rindt had departed to Lotus so Brabham was joined by Belgian Jacky Ickx, who had previously been with Ferrari. The DFV put the Brabhams back among the winners. The cars were initially unreliable but by the end of the season Ickx had won the German and Canadian GPs and finished second in the Drivers' Championship behind Stewart.

That Brabham had been hurt during a testing accident in 1969 may have spurred a decision to retire from racing, but Ickx left the team and returned to Ferrari for 1970 so, unable to sign up another driver, Brabham carried on for another season. He very nearly won yet another World Championship. 'Black Jack' won the South African GP, his last win, and picked up some places in the BT33, which was the first Tauranac-designed monocoque.

Brabham then retired and sold his interest in MRD, the Brabham holding company, to Tauranac. Double World Champion Graham Hill joined the team with Tim Schenken, an Australian who had a formidable record in Formula Ford and F3, but 1971 was a poor season with

Dan Gurney with the Brabham BT7 in the 1963 Dutch Grand Prix. He finished second.

thin results since Hill was past his best and the team was short of funds. Tauranac sold the Brabham team to Bernie Ecclestone in 1972, then returned to Australia.

Hill stayed on and was joined by Argentinian Carlos Reutemann, using the 'lobster-claw' BT34, nicknamed for its frontal aspect, but again there was little to show. Gordon Murray came from McLaren as the designer and the team picked up some places in 1973 while Murray worked to design the BT44, which was used in 1974. This was a success and gave Reutemann wins in the South African, Austrian and United States GPs. The success continued into 1975, Reutemann winning the German GP and his Brazilian team-mate, Carlos Pace, victorious in his home event. With a string of second and third places the revived Brabham came second in the Constructors' Championship.

Ecclestone wanted to find an engine with more power than the DFV – as well as one that would cost him nothing – and so he did a deal with Alfa Romeo for their flat-12 engine in 1976. The power increase was counterbalanced by the extra size and weight so little was gained. It went into a new car, the BT45, and there were many problems with the installation. There were variable power outputs and design changes made by Alfa Romeo without reference to Brabham, including changes to the engine mounting points which resulted in constant problems for the mechanics. The outcome was chaos and Reutemann walked out halfway through the season.

The 1977 season began with the popular Pace taking second place in Brazil, but he was killed in a flying accident and so the Ulster driver John Watson took over and managed another second in the French GP.

A World Champion in action. Jack Brabham on his way to victory in the 1966 British Grand Prix with the BT19.

BERNIE ECCLESTONE

Bernard 'Bernie' Ecclestone was born in 1930 and began trading in motorcycles in South London in his teens. He raced a Cooper 500 and gained some successes. In 1957 he bought a pair of B-type Connaughts when the team was closed down. He entered these for F1 events, but the cars were outclassed and the venture was unsuccessful.

Ecclestone became manager of Stuart Lewis-Evans, who had been a rival in 500 cc racing and was a member of the Vanwall team, but after Lewis-Evans's death in 1958, Ecclestone's active interest in racing waned for a while. In the late 1970s he became manager of Jochen Rindt, who was climbing the racing ladder rapidly, and also managed the Roy Winklemann team for which Rindt drove in F2. Again the management had a sad ending when Rindt was killed at Monza in 1970.

In 1972 Bernie Ecclestone bought the Brabham F1 team from Ron Tauranac. After a slow start, by 1974 the team was gaining successes. Then it suffered a setback when Ecclestone came to a deal with Alfa Romeo to supply engines which, although free, brought many problems. After reverting to the Ford-Cosworth engine success came again, followed by a successful collaboration with BMW, but when the BMW turbo engine became outclassed, Ecclestone started to lose interest in the team.

The entrepreneurial Ecclestone was the prime mover in the foundation of the Formula One Constructors' Association (FOCA) in 1972, a negotiating alliance among the teams. After he became the chief executive of FOCA in 1978, little time remained for team management. After the Brabham team was sold in 1988 Ecclestone devoted all his time to the management and growth of the F1 organisation.

Bernie's biggest coup was the Concorde Agreement, which secured the TV rights for FOCA for World Championship events. This put a large part of the TV income into the pockets of the F1 teams. Ecclestone's influence on the top echelons of motor racing has been enormous. The massive turnover and earnings generated by and for Formula 1 are largely due to his efforts.

His last win: Jack Brabham in the 1970 South African Grand Prix with the DFV-engined BT33.

Graham Hill in the 'lobster-claw' BT34 at Brands Hatch during the tragic 1971 World Championship Victory Race.

Niki Lauda, World Champion in 1977, was lured by Ecclestone into the team for 1978. Martini, the previous sponsor, was dropped and Parmalat, the Italian dairy producer, picked up the salary bill for Lauda.

Lauda gained two second places with a new BT46. Then in mid-season, at the Swedish GP, Gordon Murray produced the controversial BT46B, which used a fan to suck air from under the car and create powerful downforce. It won the race but after that was banned by the CSI, so a normal BT46 was run for the rest of the season. Lauda and Watson came first and second in the Italian GP at Monza after the two cars ahead of them had a time penalty.

For 1979 Alfa Romeo produced a V-12 engine, partly prompted by pressure from Murray who emphasised the need for a more practical unit. Also Alfa intended to use it for a return to F1 with their own car. The V-12 did not work for Brabham, the only success a win in a non-Championship race at Imola. Toward the end of the season it was mutually agreed that Brabham and Alfa Romeo would part. Then Lauda decided that motor racing had lost its charm and retired from the sport – temporarily as it would turn out.

For 1980 Brabham returned to the DFV Cosworth which was fitted to a new Murray-designed BT49. Brazilian Nelson Piquet scored three wins in the US West,

Dutch and Italian G.Ps, which gave Brabham second place in the Constructors' Championship. In 1981 there was much argument about movable skirts and ride height in F1, rules which Gordon Murray was interpreting as liberally as possible, but amid the controversy Piquet won the Argentine, San Marino and German G.Ps to take the World Championship.

Renault had shown that the long-overlooked provision in the F1 rules which allowed supercharged 1.5-litre engines was in fact exploitable, so in 1982 Ecclestone did a deal with BMW and a turbo-blown 1,500 cc BMW engine went into a new BT50; but it was a learning season and Piquet had only one win in the Canadian G.P.

Parmalat was replaced as sponsor by Fila for 1983 when the BMW engine, now in the BT52, took Piquet to a second Championship as he had won in Brazil, Austria and in the European G.P. at Brands Hatch, taking the title by a single point from Alain Prost. Italian Riccardo Patrese rounded off the season by winning in South Africa. The rival teams were getting more power from their turbo engines. To match them the BMW units became over-stressed and the Brabhams were plagued with engine failures in 1984, although Piquet scored wins in the Canadian and Detroit G.Ps.

For 1985 Ecclestone signed a contract to use Pirelli tyres. With these slightly off the pace and the engine problems continuing, the downward path of the Brabham team had begun. Piquet won the French G.P, which was the last Brabham F1 Championship victory. He left at the end of the season to join McLaren. Disputes between Brabham and BMW in 1986 about the responsibility for a dismal season intensified when Elio de Angelis was killed testing a BT55 at Paul Ricard. At the end of 1986 Murray left and joined Piquet at McLaren.

The misery continued in 1987. Ecclestone had lost interest. At the end of 1987 the MRD team was withdrawn from F1 and did not return until 1989 when the interests had been sold to the Swiss financier, Joachim Luhti. A Judd V-8 engine was used in the BT58, but it had reached a point where the cars were having difficulty in qualifying for races.

When Luhti subsequently faced charges for embezzlement, control of the team passed to the Japanese-owned Middlebridge Group.

John Watson in the 1977 flat-12 Alfa Romeo-powered BT45.

The cars now used a V-10 Judd engine and the lead driver was Graham Hill's promising son, Damon. Despite his best efforts, the shadows were closing in and the money was not there. After he took 11th place in the 1992 Hungarian G.P. it was the end of the story. Brabham had begun at the top, faltered, then made a comeback and finally just faded away.

Riccardo Patrese during the early laps of the 1982 Monaco Grand Prix with the BT49D. He went on to a lucky win after the cars in front of him ran out of fuel.

CHAPTER 16

Tyrrell and March: Kit-car Winners

THE Ford-Cosworth DFV (Double Four-Valve) opened a new era of F1 racing. The engine was conceived after it was announced that F1 would change to 3.0-litres unsupercharged in 1966. Colin Chapman approached Mike Costin and Keith Duckworth whose engines, built by their company Cosworth Engineering at Northampton on a basis of Ford parts, had dominated Formula Junior and Formula 2 from 1960.

They said they could build Chapman a suitable engine to power the F1 Lotus but would need £100,000 to do the job, which included the 1.6-litre four-cylinder FVA engine for Formula 2. Chapman bustled round and raised the sponsorship from the Ford Motor Company, which was already deeply involved with motor sport in a campaign to give Ford a new, more sporting image. In return for the sponsorship the Ford name was emblazoned on the cam boxes of the 3.0-litre V-8 DFV.

Lotus had the exclusive use of the DFV in 1967. It was soon evident that it was superior to any other engine in F1 and Ford said it would be available for other car manufacturers to buy for the 1968 season. The other essential specialist component in a racing car was the gearbox, which also had a willing supplier. Hewland Engineering at Maidenhead in the Thames Valley had started making gearboxes for rear-engined cars based on VW components when Formula Junior began. The use of the Hewland box was almost universal.

Aware of the need for a suitable gearbox to mate with the V-8 Coventry Climax engine, Hewland entered the F1 field and was ready for the 3.0-litre formula with its new DG300 unit. With off-the-shelf engines and gearboxes available, it became possible for a team with sponsorship, a competent designer and a good workshop to make a competitive F1 car and enter the fray.

One such entrant was Ken Tyrrell. Born in 1924, Tyrrell owned a timber yard at Ripley, a village south-west of London. He was a successful competitor in the 500 cc class, driving a Cooper in the early 1950s, moving on to a sports T39 Cooper and then into F2. Tyrrell gave up racing in 1959 to become the manager and owner of a team which was effectively the Cooper works Formula Junior team. Renowned as a talent-spotter, between 1960 and 1964 he introduced John Surtees and Jackie Stewart to single-seater racing in his FJ Coopers.

Stewart joined the BRM F1 team in 1965 and Tyrrell continued running Coopers in F2. When approached by the French aerospace company, Matra, he agreed to run an F2 Matra with Stewart as the driver in 1966 and 1967. To their mutual surprise the Matra chassis turned out to

The March 701 being shown to the press in the spring of 1970.

Tyrrell

be quite good. Matra moved up to F1 in 1968 using the DFV engine, supplying a car to Tyrrell for whom Stewart was the number one driver.

In 1969 there was real success as Stewart was World Champion and Matra won the Constructors' Championship. In 1970 Matra wanted Tyrrell to use their V-12 engine, but he was not keen and decided to build his own F1 car for Stewart. Since it was not going to be ready to race until the end of the 1970 season, he had to find an alternative car meanwhile.

Tyrrell found his alternative at Bicester near Silverstone. March Engineering was formed in 1969 by Max Mosley, Alan Rees, Graham Coaker and Robin Herd. Their aim was to manufacture racing cars for sale, primarily for F2 and F3 but also for F1, if customers

could be found. Mosley was the commercial brain, Herd designed the cars, Rees supervised the racing and Coaker looked after the production in a factory at Bicester.

Herd came up with an orthodox F1 design, the March 701, based around the DFV engine and the Hewland gearbox. Paying with Ford money, Ken Tyrrell ordered three for the 1970 season which were painted blue. As Stewart won the Spanish G.P. it looked good for March, but after that the results were less happy and there were no more wins either by the Tyrrell cars or by the works team.

Tyrrell's own car, built in a workshop at Ockham not far from the timber yard, was designed by Derek Gardner, whose previous work had been mainly in transmissions. Ready at the end of 1970, it was a conventional F1 design

Jackie Stewart in the Tyrrell 001 at the 1970 United States Grand Prix.

Ronnie Peterson with the March 711 at Monaco in 1971.

Ken Tyrrell (left) and Derek Gardner, the designer, stand behind the P34. Patrick Depailler is in the car.

JACKIE STEWART

Jackie Stewart was born in 1939 into a motor racing family, for his elder brother Jimmy drove for Ecurie Ecosse in the early 1950s. Stewart drove for the same Scottish team in 1963 after beginning in club racing. His big break came in 1964 when he joined the F3 Cooper team run by Ken Tyrrell, effectively the works team. His domination of F3 in 1964 led to an F1 deal with BRM for 1965. He scored his first Championship win at Monza in 1965.

He stayed with BRM in 1966 and 1967, but suffered from the team's disorganisation and so was happy to go back to Tyrrell in 1968 and drive a Matra-Cosworth. His several F1 wins were a harbinger of the success of the Tyrrell/Stewart/Matra combination in 1969 when Stewart won his first World Championship.

Starting 1970 with a March-DFV was not quite so successful. Stewart waited while Tyrrell developed his own F1 car and his patience was rewarded with a second World Championship in 1971 in the Tyrrell-Ford. A stomach ulcer held Stewart back in 1972, but there was a third Championship in 1973. He had decided to retire

at the end of 1973 and his decision was confirmed when his Tyrrell team-mate Cevert was killed in practice for the American G.P.

Jackie Stewart had been very concerned at the number of his fellow drivers who had been killed while racing. Starting in 1966, when he was appalled by his treatment after a crash at Spa, and into retirement, he devoted himself to working for higher safety standards in racing and particularly in F1. The relative safety of current F1 can be traced back to Stewart's efforts, which were not always understood or appreciated at the time.

In retirement the Scotsman has dedicated much time in support of charities. He returned to an active interest in F1 in 1997 when, with his son Paul, he formed the Stewart team, with much support from Ford. After only moderate success the Stewart team was bought by Ford at the end of 1999 to be transformed into Jaguar, again wearing the green. Stewart's charitable work, his efforts to make racing safer and his triple Championships were recognised when he was knighted in 2001.

using the DFV and the Hewland gearbox. The team, still in blue livery, was sponsored by Elf, the French oil company. Stewart swept the board in 1971, winning the Spanish, Monaco, French, British, German and Canadian G.Ps to become World Champion. His team-mate, young Frenchman Francois Cevert, backed up well with a string of places and a win in the US G.P. to gain Tyrrell the Constructors' Championship.

For March it was a different story as Robin Herd's new design, the 711, was not competitive. The chances of Stewart and Tyrrell repeating their success in 1972 were diminished by Stewart's illness with a stomach ulcer, but he won the Argentine, French, Canadian and US G.Ps to come second in the Championship behind Fittipaldi's Lotus.

Stewart was fully back to form in 1973, winning the South African, Monaco, Belgian, Dutch and German G.Ps to take the title again. His triumph was marred as Cevert was killed in a crash during practice for the US G.P, from which Tyrrell withdrew Stewart's car as a symbol of respect. Stewart then retired from the sport and Tyrrell, who had won a second Constructors' Championship, had to find all-new drivers for 1974.

March meanwhile was soldiering on in F1, using a car developed from the F2 chassis. It had enough promise for James Hunt to pick up some places and be beaten in the US G.P. by a scant 0.3 second. It was even better in F2, though, as the March 732 with the BMW M12 engine was most successful and Jean-Pierre 'Jumper' Jarier was European F2 Champion.

Ken Tyrrell signed up the relatively inexperienced South African Jody Scheckter, who showed his ability by winning the Swedish and British G.Ps in the new Tyrrell 007, designed by Gardner. Like the Lotus 72 it had had torsion-bar suspension, unlike the coil springs of the conventional 'British kit car'. Again it was a miserable F1 season for March, but Patrick Depailler, who had the number two Tyrrell seat in F1, was the European F2 Champion in a works March 732.

For 1975 Gardner went back to coil springs as the torsion bars were difficult to adjust, but the results were more patchy with the only win in South Africa. A slight upturn in March fortunes was a win for Vittorio Brambilla in a works March 751 in the Austrian G.P, albeit the race was stopped just after half-distance when the track was flooded with torrential rain.

The March 240 which was built in 1977 but never raced.

Ken Tyrrell (right), shakes the hand of Paul Murphy of Candy Domestic Appliances Ltd, the main sponsors of the unsuccessful 1979 Tyrrell 009.

BRANDS HATCH began as a grass track for motorcycle racing in the 1930s. In 1950 the one mile course was given a permanent surface and became the centre of activity for the rapidly growing 500 cc racing class. The 500 cc cars used the circuit exclusively until the Druids Hill extension was built in 1954, lengthening the distance to 1.25 miles. Still in use, this circuit is known as the Indy Circuit.

The circuit, agreeably set in a natural amphitheatre, rapidly gained in stature. Meetings were held continuously throughout the year, even on Boxing Day. By the end of the 1950s full international F2 meetings were being held, attended by all the major teams and drivers. In 1960 the circuit was extended again, doubling its length to 2.3 miles with an undulating loop through the woods south of the original circuit.

Its extension, known as the Grand Prix Circuit, made Brands Hatch suitable for long-distance sports car events and non-Championship F1 races. After 1964, when the British G.P. was run at Brands Hatch, the circuit became a venue for the G.P. in alternate years until 1986.

The Grand Prix circuit continues to be used for major touring and sports car races while the Indy Circuit is a major venue for club meetings. Many famous drivers raced for the first time at Brands Hatch.

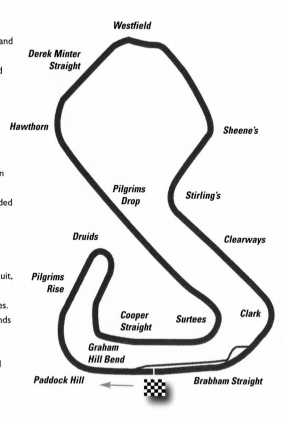

For the 1976 season Derek Gardner produced one of the most unconventional designs ever to appear in F1. The Tyrrell P34 had six wheels with two pairs at the front and a single pair at the rear. The intention was to reduce the frontal area with the small front wheels and give better braking. To the surprise of the sceptics, it worked. Scheckter and Depailler took first and second places in the Swedish G.P. and during the season picked up another eight second places to give Tyrrell third place in the Constructors' Championship.

March was still trying. Robin Herd too had flirted with the idea of a six-wheel car, with the double pair in the rear, but had abandoned it. Blond Swede Ronnie Peterson was the number one driver and the March 761 was the fastest car in the field, though plagued with unreliability. Peterson won the 1976 Italian G.P, which was to be the last F1 win for March. After that, the marque had little impact on F1 for nearly a decade.

The development of the Tyrrell was frustrated by a lack of suitable tyres for the tiny front wheels. After a poor season in 1977 the design was abandoned and Gardner departed. His place was taken by Maurice Phillippe, who designed a conventional car for 1978, the 008, which gave Depailler a win at Monaco. That was the last Tyrrell success for some time.

Phillippe produced a series of cars which gained places but not until the end of the 1982 season did a win come for the Italian Michele Alboreto in the Las Vegas G.P. in a 011. The 011 was re-vamped for 1983, when Alboreto won the United States (East) G.P, but that was to be the last win for Tyrrell and also the last win for the DFV Ford-Cosworth engine.

By now the better-off teams were making full use of the 1.5-litre turbocharged engines allowed by the rules, but it was a development which Ken Tyrrell could not afford. Worse was to come. After a fuel test showed that the Tyrrells were running with an illegal additive, the team was barred from the 1984 Championship. Tyrrell never fully recovered from this setback.

In the following seasons Renault, Ford, Honda, Ilmor and Yamaha engines were used. Some minor places were gained; the best being two seconds scored by Franco-Italian, Jean Alesi, with an 019 designed by Harvey Postlethwaite, in the US and Monaco G.Ps in 1990. There was not enough sponsorship money in an evermore expensive sport. In 1998 Ken Tyrrell who, by now, was a sick man, sold the team to British-American Tobacco and it became BAR. Tyrrell died in 2001 after a long illness.

Although by the mid-1970s March was having no success in F1, the company itself was flourishing and had become one of the leading makers of cars for other formulas. Bruno Giacomelli dominated F2 in 1978 and was the European Champion with a March 782, while Marc Surer continued this dominance in 1979.

In 1981 March moved into the lucrative US market with the 81C, a development of the F1 FW07, which was designed for Indianapolis and CART (Championship Auto Racing Teams) racing. Using a DFX Cosworth engine, the car was soon a success, bringing the downforce concept to American racing. The first win in 1981 came at Pocono, with A. J. Foyt as the driver. The major breakthrough came in 1983 when an 83C, driven by Tony Sneva, won the Indianapolis 500.

Led by the canny Robin Herd, March soon dominated American racing. Almost incredibly, in 1984 its 84Cs with Cosworth engines took the first 14 places in the Indy 500. Indy success was repeated in 1985, 1986 and 1987. March also built a series of cars for Group 7 sports car

Bobby Rahal in a March 83C Cosworth.
A similar car won the 1984 Indianapolis 500
driven by Rick Mears.

racing. One of these, an 83G with a 3.2-litre Porsche engine, won the Daytona 24-hour race in 1984, a round in the World Endurance Championship Triple Crown. There was a return to F1 in 1987. An 881 with a Judd engine, designed by Adrian Newey, was competitive during the 1988 season taking a second place in Portugal.

By the mid-1980s Robin Herd was the only member of the founding quartet still remaining with March. His efforts were rewarded by his appointment as a CBE in the 1987 New Year's Honours list. March was floated as a public company in 1987, but major financial problems erupted almost immediately with a slump in US sales. Japanese interests bought a substantial part of the March assets in 1989, allowing F1 participation to continue until 1993 through the Leyton House team, but there

was no success. The March name disappeared from motor racing.

Ken Tyrrell and his team achieved remarkable results on limited assets. The Tyrrell team was run in the style of a private team of the 1950s and 1960s. As soon as the bigger teams could allocate multi-million budgets for research and development alone, there was no more room for Tyrrell.

After its first season March failed to make a real impact on F1, but the company gained huge prestige for Britain in the lesser formulae and in its domination of CART racing in the United States. In all 1,457 Marches were built. Neither Tyrrell nor March was ever seen in true British Racing Green but both waved the flag magnificently.

CHAPTER 17

Lola: Mass-produced Success

LOLA is the world's most prolific racing car manufacturer. No other organisation has produced such a wide range of competition cars and in such numbers, waving the Union Jack at circuits around the world.

Its story had small beginnings. In 1957 Eric Broadley, a quantity surveyor, built a Ford-engined special to compete in the 1172 formula class of the 750 Club. He dubbed it 'Lola' after the song 'Whatever Lola wants, Lola gets' from the 1950s musical 'Damn Yankees'. Encouraged by its success, Broadley built a neat 1,100 cc Climax-engined sports car, the Mark 1, which quickly toppled Lotus from its dominance of the small sports car class.

The Mark 1's success brought in orders and Broadley formed Lola Cars Ltd in a small works in Bromley, on the southern outskirts of London, and began production. The series-built Mk 1s gained many victories. When Formula Junior commenced in England in 1959, Broadley made the Mk 2. Though beautifully engineered this was not quick enough to beat the rear-engined Lotus 18 so in 1961 the next FJ Lola had the engine behind the driver.

Broadley's ability and the quality of his Lola were soon recognised. In 1962 the Bowmaker finance company commissioned an F1 design, the Lola T4, using the V-8 1.5-litre Coventry Climax engine. The Bowmaker team had John Surtees and Roy Salvadori as drivers. The results were modest although Surtees took second place in the British and German GPs. Bowmaker pulled out of racing after only a season.

With other projects in hand Lola's direct interest in F1 diminished, but in 1967 Surtees, who had then joined Honda, approached Broadley for help. With its V-12 engine the F1 Honda RA273 was too heavy and so Broadley modified a T90 chassis, which had originally been built for USAC racing, and this became the Honda 300. In a slip-streaming drama, so often seen at Monza, Surtees won the 1967 Italian GP to give Honda its only victory in the original 3.0-litre Formula 1. A development, the Honda 301, with much input from Broadley, was raced in 1968.

The demand for its cars was such that the company had out-grown the small Bromley works. Lola moved to a factory at Slough, west of London, where Broadley designed a Ford-powered mid-engined sports-racing coupé in 1962. After an initial appearance at Le Mans, the design was bought by the Ford Motor Co. to become a test horse for development of its hugely successful GT 40, variants of which were to win at Le Mans four times. Broadley's works was turned over to Ford Advanced Vehicles, producer of the original GT40 in series.

The Ford project slowed Lola's own developments for over a year, but the GT was followed in 1965 by the Lola T70, a sports-racing car with a V-8 Chevrolet engine and Hewland transaxle. This was immediately successful in the popular and wealthy Can-Am series of races held in Canada and the United States, taking Surtees to the 1966 Can-Am Championship.

Jack Brabham's drive at Indianapolis in 1961, followed by Jim Clark's domination of the 1964 500-mile race until tyre failure intervened, made Broadley appreciate the possibilities of the American racing market. Similarly, American teams scrambled to find Britons who understood this new-fangled rear-engined lark. The Ford-powered T80 was produced and Al Unser took it to 9th place in the 1965 '500'. In 1966 Lola was at Indianapolis in force with two of the new T90s minded by ace Indy mechanic, George Bignotti, and driven by BRM team-mates Graham Hill and Jackie Stewart.

After 192 of the race's 200 laps Stewart led by over a lap when his engine lost oil pressure. He pulled off and Hill went on to take the lucrative victory. Between 1965 and 1970 several Lola seconds and thirds were gained at Indianapolis, but the win was not repeated. Meanwhile the T70 had been developed into a GT coupé which found a ready market. In 1969 Mark Donohue and Chuck Parsons took a T70 to victory in the Daytona 24-hours. On a lower level Denny Hulme won the 1968 Tourist Trophy at Oulton Park with a T70.

For the 2.0-litre sports-racing class, which was becoming significant in the early 1970s, Lola produced its T212 with an FVA Cosworth engine. It became a prominent competitor. In 1972 the Sports Car World Championship rules were changed, with the aim of bringing it into line with F1 by reducing the allowable engine size to 3.0 litres. The T212 had been succeeded by the T290, a modified version of which was fitted with a 3.0-litre DFV V-8 Cosworth to become the T280, to exploit this opportunity.

Like almost every Lola car the T280 was raced not as a works entry but by independent teams with factory support. It was fast but unreliable so there were no notable results. The successes continued in the 2.0-litre class, however, with the T292, T294, and T296, developments of the T290 design. Many of these were fitted with other units such as BMW and Alfa Romeo by European customers.

Lola approached F2 in much the same manner as F1 had been tackled. Various models were produced for the 1.0-litre F2, which ended in 1966, but there was only a modicum of success. When F2 was changed to a 1.6 litre

limit in 1967, BMW commissioned a chassis, the T100, to take its radial-valved engine. Although this was not quick enough with the heavy and peaky BMW engine, other entrants scored wins using the FVA Cosworth.

Lola moved from Slough to a new factory at Huntingdon in 1970, partly prompted by moves to the same location by Progress Chassis and Specialised Mouldings who made the Lola frames and bodies. From the new factory came the next F1 venture in 1974. After leaving Lotus, Graham Hill launched his own F1 team with sponsorship from Embassy Tobacco. Hill commissioned Lola to build an F1 car.

Although handsome, like almost all Lolas, it was a typical 'kit car' with a conventional chassis using a Cosworth DFV engine and a Hewland gearbox. The T370 was not successful. Hill was past his best while Guy Edwards and Rolf Stommelen were not top-line drivers and so the cars were mostly back-markers during the 1974 and 1975 seasons. The T370 project ended after Hill was killed in a flying accident in November 1975.

Although F1 success still eluded Lola, the story was different in F5000, the class for stock-block V-8-engined

The sports Lola Mk 1, seen here being driven by Stirling Moss in an historic race at Silverstone in 1994.

John Surtees in the 1962 F1 Lola T4.

single-seaters which had been introduced in the late 1960s. After initial successes with the T140, the T330 was introduced in 1972. The British driver, Brian Redman, dominated the Formula A/5000 class in the United States, winning the SCCA/USAC Championship in 1974, 1975 and 1976.

Lola returned to Indianapolis in 1978. In an entry by Texan Jim Hall of Chaparral fame, Al Unser won the 500-mile race in a T500 with a Cosworth engine, the first all-British car to win the race. He also won the Ontario and Pocono '500s.

While supporting the upper echelons of the sport, the main business of Lola was building cars for the lesser formulas. The T200 designed for Formula Ford, the nursery racing class, sold well and scored many wins. Cars were also built for the Sports 2000 category and the lowly, but popular, Formula Vee.

In the early 1980s Lola received a commission from Nissan to build a Group C sports-racing car, the T810,

The Lola GT which served as a test bed for concepts used in the Ford GT 40, seen when it was introduced at the 1962 Racing Car Show.

1966 Lola T90

The Lola T90 powered by a Ford engine, and entered by American John Mecom, was the second British car to win the 'Indy 500' when Graham Hill took the flag in 1966. It was a lucky win for Hill as his team-mate, Jackie Stewart, also in a T90, was in the lead with only eight laps to go, but stopped with a broken engine, almost in sight of victory.

Dan Gurney with a Lola T160 in the 1968 Can-Am Riverside race.

as Haas-Lolas but had a negligible impact on the F1 scene.

A much more serious involvement arose in 1987 when the French driver Gérard Larousse assembled an F1 team with sponsorship from the French financier Didier Calmels. A Lola chassis was used. The LC87, designed by Ralph Bellamy, was of carbon composite construction and used a 3.5-litre Cosworth DFX. Driven by Phillippe Alliot and Yannick Dalmas, the cars picked up a handful of points during the season, but the 3.0-litre DFX lacked the power of the 1.5-litre turbo-blown cars which were dominating F1.

The cars were updated for 1988, becoming the LC88. Bellamy had departed after a disagreement and so its development was done by Chris Murphy, but it was a poor season and no World Championship points were gained. The chassis was reworked again for 1989 by Gérard Decarouge and Murphy to accommodate a V-12 Lamborghini engine which used a transverse gearbox; the wheelbase was lengthened and the car became the LC88B. A new car, the LC89, came out in mid-season.

Once again the results were insignificant. The Larousse team also had financial problems as backer Calmels was in prison, convicted of shooting his wife. Murphy produced the LC90 for the 1990 season. With drivers Eric Bernard and Aguri Suzuki the team had a reasonable season, placing sixth in the Constructors' Championship ahead of such declining notables as Lotus and Brabham, but the team was struck out of the Championship for a technical infringement.

Larousse switched to the turbo Cosworth DFR engine for 1991. This was fitted to the LC91, designed by Broadley himself, but reliability was a rare commodity. Two sixth places were all that could be achieved. At the end of 1991 Larousse abandoned Lola and moved over to the French-built Venturi chassis.

While F1 was proving a hard struggle, Lola enjoyed further glory in the United States. In 1990 the Dutch driver, Arie Luyendyk, won the Indy 500 with a Chevrolet-powered T90/00 while Al Unser won the Indycar Championship. In 1991 Michael Andretti took the CART/PPG title while Bobby Rahal was the Indycar

using the V-6 Nissan engine as a power unit. The Nissans raced regularly from 1985 to 1989 and gained some places. Notable success came in the United States where Geoff Brabham, son of Champion Jack, won the 1988 and 1989 IMSA Championships. The Lola-built Nissan R90C was probably the fastest Group C car racing in 1990, but although several seconds and thirds were scored, there was no outright win.

In 1981 a new sports Lola, the T600, was built for the Endurance Drivers Championship. A descendant of the T280, it had a DFV Cosworth engine. The T600 was successful in a season characterised by rather thin entries. Driven by Briton Guy Edwards and the Spanish driver, Emilio de Vilotta, it scored wins in the Six-Hour Coppa Florio at Enna in Sicily and in the Brands Hatch 1000 kms race. Across the Atlantic a Chevrolet-powered T600 came second in the Mosport Six Hours and in the Elkhart Lake '500'.

In name at least Lola was back in F1 for the 1985 season, when a new team was sponsored by the American Beatrice Corporation conglomerate. The cars, called Beatrice-Lola, used a 1.5-litre turbo Cosworth V-6 engine, but there was little input from the Huntingdon factory as the cars were built elsewhere. In 1986 the cars raced again

JOHN SURTEES

John Surtees holds the unique distinction of being the only man to be World Champion in both motor racing and motorcycle racing. Surtees was born in 1934. His father was a successful motorcycle racer and young John followed him, starting in 1951. Between 1956 and 1960 he won seven World motorcycle titles in the 350 cc and 500 cc classes, riding for Norton and MV Agusta.

Surtees began racing cars in 1960, initially driving a Tyrrell-owned FJ Cooper, but such was his obvious talent that by the end of the season he was a full member of Team Lotus in F1. Two poor years followed in the private Yeoman Credit team with a Cooper and with the first F1 Lola. In 1963 Surtees signed with Ferrari and scored his first Championship win in the German G.P. In 1964 he was World Champion, getting the result with two wins and some consistent places.

This career trajectory was interrupted in 1965, when Surtees was badly hurt in a crash

with a Can-Am Lola. He stayed with Ferrari until the middle of the 1966 season when the politics of the Italian factory forced his departure. He went to Cooper for the rest of 1966, gaining a rare win for the Cooper-Maserati.

Profiting from his motorcycle connections, Surtees joined Honda in 1967, but spent more time developing the car than gaining success and so there was only one F1 win. A sojourn with BRM in 1969 was unhappy, so Surtees decided to follow the path of Brabham and McLaren and build his own F1 car.

The Formula 1 Surtees was a typical F1 kit car using a DFV Ford-Cosworth engine. John drove himself until 1972, but neither he nor his team gained the success of the eponymous rivals. Team Surtees continued in F1 until the end of 1978, when the lack of success and sponsorship forced a withdrawal. Surtees still takes an active interest in historic racing.

champion using the T91/00. In 1991, when Lola took second to eighth places in the Indy 500, 28 of the 33 starters were Lolas. The 1992 season saw World Champion Nigel Mansell leave F1 and join the Indycar circus for 1993, sensationally taking the Championship in a T93/00.

After only a year away Lola returned to F1 in 1993, joining forces with BMS Scuderia Italia to produce the T93/30, powered by a V-12 Ferrari engine. It was an unmitigated disaster. Michele Alboreto and Luca Badoer failed to qualify, retired or finished at the back of the field, many laps behind. Sadly, worse was to come.

In 1996 Lola made a fateful decision. After nearly forty years in the sport it made a direct company entry into F1 for the first time, with MasterCard as the sponsor. The T97/30 was produced with a Cosworth ED V-8. Lola had intended to delay racing until 1998 to allow time for development, but pressure from the sponsors was such that two cars were brought out for the 1997 season. Driven by Italian Vincenzo Sospiro and Brazilian Ricardo Rosset, the cars appeared for the Australian G.P, but were hopelessly uncompetitive and failed to qualify.

The highly public failure had dramatic repercussions. With MasterCard not having met its commitments, Lola founder Eric Broadley decided to call a halt to the abortive

effort. With no recoupment of its F1 investment Lola was in severe financial difficulty. The company went into receivership, from which the assets were bought by ex-Lola driver Martin Birrane. He re-formed the company; racing car production began again, and Lola moved into a much wider commercial field, drawing on the new wind tunnel that Broadley had commissioned and the huge technological expertise which the founder had established over the years.

In 1985 Formula 3000 was established as a kind of F2 successor, a stepping stone for drivers who had aspirations to enter F1. Initially this used DFV Cosworth engines but other units were also used in chassis which Lola manufactured, based on the Indy design. In 1996 it was decided that F3000 should become a one-make class. Lola was the selected builder, its cars being fitted with Judd-based Zytek V-8 engines.

Lola provided cars for F3000 until the end of 2004, when it was replaced by the GP2 class using Dallara chassis. Lola bounced back with a contract to build cars for the new A1GP series, for national teams racing in a world-wide circus. Commencing in 2005, it used a Lola chassis.

After many years Lola returned to F3 in 2006 with its successful B06/30. At its Huntingdon base the company continues to produce cars for almost every international

LOLA

The Lola T70, which won the 1969 Daytona 24-hours driven by Mark Donohue and Chuck Parsons, makes a night pit stop.

Brian Redman in the Lola T330 with which he won the SCCA/USAC Championships in 1974, 1975 and 1976.

The first all-British Indy win. Al Unser in his victorious T500 Cosworth in 1978. Jim Hall, the entrant, is on the right.

A Lola T90/50 F3000 of 1990.

formula. Its wind tunnel and technical services are also exploited by leading F1 teams.

Only in Formula 1 has success eluded Lola. In every other racing field its cars have achieved outstanding results. Since its beginnings in 1958 over 2,000 competition cars have been built, a number greatly exceeding the comparable production of any other manufacturer. Though ironically only seldom wearing the green, Lolas have gained huge prestige for Britain throughout the World.

CHAPTER 18

Williams: Triumph over Adversity

Sir Frank Williams

SON of an RAF bomber pilot, Frank Williams was born at South Shields in the north-east of England in 1942. He began racing an Austin A40 saloon in 1962, then moved on to Formula 3. In 1968 he began managing a Brabham F2 team and among his paying drivers was Max Mosley, now President of the FIA.

Outstanding among those who drove for Williams was Piers Courage, scion of a brewing family. In 1969 Williams entered F1 with a Brabham BT26 in which Courage took promising second places in the Monaco and United States G.Ps. For 1970 Williams turned to the Argentinean Alejandro de Tomaso who produced an F1 car with the ubiquitous Ford DFV engine. Sadly Courage crashed it in the Dutch G.P. and was killed.

Though deeply affected, Williams showed his grit by carrying on. With sponsorship from the oil company Motul and from Politoys, a March 721 was run in 1972. A new car, the FX3, was built in a small workshop at Reading, engineered by Len Bailey who had done much of the design work on the Ford GT40. This Politoys-FX3 made little impression.

For 1973 Williams found new sponsorship from tobacco company Marlboro and Italian car maker Iso and so the reworked FX3-Ford was known as the Iso-Marlboro. After little success both Iso and Marlboro pulled out and so 1974 found Williams scratching around, borrowing and buying parts from other teams to survive.

A new car designed by Ray Stokoe for the 1975 season became the Williams FW04. This ran with the old FX3. At the end of that season an Austrian entrepreneur, Walter Wolf, bought a controlling interest in the Williams team. Following a disastrous season for Wolf-Williams in 1976, Frank Williams departed to found Williams Grand Prix Engineering in a small works at Didcot. His designer was Patrick Head, who had joined Wolf from McLaren.

Head designed the FW06, a practical, conventional Ford-powered car driven in 1978 by the Australian, Alan Jones. Sponsorship came from Saudi Airlines, whose colours of green and white happily restored green to a British racing car. The season ended on an upward trend with a second place in the US G.P. The FW06 was used at the beginning of the 1979 season, when Jones was joined by the Italian, Clay Regazzoni, but Head was working on a new design.

Patrick Head had not only seen, but also understood, the results achieved by Lotus with 'ground effect' in 1978. He pursued this approach with the FW07 which appeared in mid-season. After a slow start it all came good at Silverstone when the FW07s dominated the race and

Regazzoni won easily. Jones then scored a hat-trick in winning the German, Austrian and Dutch G.Ps and finished 1979 by leading Regazzoni home in a 1-2 in the United States G.P. Williams was second to Ferrari in the Constructors' Championship. In just three years, greatly aided by the brilliance of Head's design, Frank Williams had come from being the pauper of F1 to a dominant player.

It came even better in 1980 with the FW07B, which had been improved and refined by Head in a rapidly expanding factory at Didcot, where research and development were given a high priority. The second car was driven by Argentinian Carlos Reutemann who won at Monaco, but the 'take no prisoners' Jones was the driver to beat. He won the Argentine, French, British, Italian, Canadian and US G.Ps to become World Champion, while Williams took the Constructors' title.

The beginning of 1981 saw open controversy between the manufacturers and the ruling body, FISA, over sliding skirts to aid ground effect. When the skirts were banned, Head made quick changes to the FW07C to make it legal. Jones won the US West and US G.Ps while Reutemann won in Brazil and Belgium. Mistakes and tensions at the end of the season cost the Argentinian the World Championship, lost by a single point to Brabham-mounted Piquet. Their results gave Williams the Constructors' title again – an honour the team highly esteemed – by a wide margin.

The year 1982 was disappointing. Jones, disillusioned with the skirt furore, had retired from F1 and the season began with the FW07Cs driven by Reutemann and the Finn, Keke Rosberg. After two races, Reutemann walked out to give up racing, leaving Rosberg in the number one seat. It was an unhappy Championship season marred by the death of Gilles Villeneuve. Rosberg drove consistently and at the end was World Champion by virtue of his consistent scoring although he only won once, in the Swiss G.P. held at Dijon. Williams was fourth in the Constructors' title race.

Patrick Head had continued aerodynamic progress, using a new wind tunnel at Didcot. Head, like Tyrrell and March, had studied the possibility of a six-wheeled car. A prototype was built and tested and looked promising, but six-wheelers were banned in 1983 – although the six-wheeler's tub formed the basis of the FW08, which appeared in the middle of the season.

1.5-litre blown engines had come to F1, leaving Williams no longer competitive with the unblown DFV. An agreement was reached with Honda to use its 1.5-litre V-6. The delivery of engines took longer than

The 1979 FW07 Williams.

expected and so for 1983 the team carried on with the DFV, scoring one win for Rosberg at Monaco. That autumn the Williams organisation moved into a large new factory, still at Didcot. Despite Honda power, 1984 was a poor year and Rosberg could win only one Championship race at Dallas, while his French team-mate, Jacques Lafitte, had little to show.

The FW10, designed by Head for 1985, was an innovation as it used a carbon-fibre tub instead of the aluminium honeycomb used previously, and Honda supplied an up-rated engine. Saudi had been replaced as the major sponsor by Canon, and Rosberg was joined by moustachioed Nigel Mansell. It was a much better year. Rosberg won the United States and German G.Ps while Mansell, who took time to find his feet, finished the season with back-to-back wins in the European G.P. at Brands Hatch and in South Africa with an improved FW10B.

In March of 1986 the Williams team was hit by a personal disaster. After testing at the Paul Ricard circuit near Marseilles, Frank Williams was returning to Nice airport in a hired car when he went off the road. His injuries left him permanently paralysed below the arms. There were doubts whether the team would or even could continue, but with great courage and determination

Nigel Mansell in the 1987 FW11B.

Frank Williams adapted his life to the disability and the team carried on.

When Rosberg went to McLaren the team was joined by another World Champion, Nelson Piquet, who had taken the 1981 and 1983 titles. With the V-6 Honda on song and the FW11, a developed FW10B, Williams took the Constructors' title again, secured by Mansell's wins in Belgium, Canada, France, Britain and Portugal, while Piquet took the flag in Brazil, Germany, Hungary and Italy. Frank Williams had the most powerful driver pairing in F1. They made that point forcefully in 1987 when Piquet took the World title with Mansell as runner-up. The Constructors' title went to Williams, amassing almost double the points of second-place McLaren.

Frank Williams's achievements in F1, combined with his fight-back from disability, were recognised when he was appointed a CBE in 1987, but political storm clouds were gathering around Didcot. Piquet left at the end of 1987 to drive for Lotus, also a Honda user, while Ayrton Senna had moved from Lotus to McLaren, taking Honda support with him. Thus Honda were supplying engines to three teams.

Relations between Williams and Honda, which had become strained despite the successes, came to a head when Honda announced it wished to nominate the second driver for 1988. Williams would not accept this – the team has always fiercely valued its independence – so the contract to supply engines was terminated.

A new engine source had to be found quickly. Williams used the 3.5-litre Judd V-8 for the 1988 season, but the results were dismal and a dispirited Mansell left for Ferrari. The F1 rules changed in 1989: turbos were barred and engines had to be unsupercharged with a maximum capacity of 3.5 litres. Renault supplied a new V-10 to Williams, whose fortunes improved. Belgian Thierry Boutsen won in Canada and Australia and was backed up by Riccardo Patrese; their efforts took Williams to second place in the Constructors' table.

The following year, using the FW13, Boutsen won in Hungary and Patrese was victorious at Imola. Mansell came back to Williams in 1991. Joining Patrese, he scored a hat-trick of successive wins in the French, British and German G.Ps and also took the Italian and Spanish G.Ps, while Patrese scored

NIGEL MANSELL

Nigel Mansell was born in Worcestershire in 1953. After racing karts – increasingly a nursery for F1 drivers – he moved into Formula Ford in 1976 and became British Formula Ford Champion in 1977. Bravely, Mansell abandoned his job as an aerospace engineer to become a professional.

He raced in Formula 3 in 1978-79 with little success. Despite this, Mansell was noticed by Colin Chapman and joined Team Lotus in 1980, initially as a test driver but soon as a regular F1 driver. He had little success in his five seasons with Lotus, spoiling several likely wins through errors.

In 1985 Mansell joined Williams, ending his season with two wins. In 1986 he enjoyed a good year with five F1 wins. Mansell started the last race of the season in Australia with a chance of the Championship only to crash after a tyre failure. It was much the same story in 1987; there were six wins but Championship hopes were lost after he was injured in a practice crash before the last round in Japan.

After Williams broke with Honda in 1988 Mansell had a poor season with an uncompetitive car and bolted to Ferrari in 1989, the last driver signed personally by Enzo Ferrari before his death. His two seasons with Ferrari saw only three wins and many retirements. Ferrari signed Alain Prost for 1991, so Mansell, feeling there was not room in the team for both of them, went back to Williams. The Williams-Renault was fully competitive and Mansell scored five times to be Championship runner-up.

His year was 1992. Mansell won nine rounds to become World Champion and also the hero of the British racing public, who admired his gritty determination. A disagreement with Williams over terms saw Mansell leave F1 in 1993 and go to the USA to race in the CART Indy series. It was a worthwhile change as he became the CART Champion in 1993, but problems and disagreements made 1994 a poor US season for him.

Mansell returned to Williams halfway through the 1994 season after Ayrton Senna's death and ended the season with his final F1 win in Australia. After two races for McLaren in 1995 he retired from F1. In retirement Mansell has tended his business interests, including a golfing estate. He drove in the short-lived GP Masters series in 2005 and has had occasional outings in GT cars.

---

in Mexico and Portugal; so Williams were back on form again.

Nineteen ninety-two was the *annus mirabilis* for Williams. The V-10 Renault was at its peak; Head, who had been joined by aerodynamicist Adrian Newey, produced the FW14B and Mansell won nine of the 16 Championship rounds, taking the title, while another win went to Patrese. Williams again took the Constructors' title with almost double the points of McLaren, the runner-up.

When Mansell could not agree terms for 1993 and left to try his luck in the United States, his seat was taken by Alain Prost, the Champion in 1985, 1986 and 1989. Mansell's departure was Prost's gain. The Frenchman took his fourth title in the FW15C, winning eight Championship rounds, while Damon Hill, Graham's son who had taken the second seat, scored a hat-trick of wins. Williams ended the season taking the Constructors' title once again with wins in eleven of the 16 rounds.

As if in some Faustian bargain, the triumphs of 1993 were paid for by tragedy in 1994. Having signed Ayrton Senna, the champion in 1988, 1990 and 1991, Williams had a powerful driver set-up with Hill in the other car. In the fourth Championship round at Imola, Senna crashed and was killed. Hill carried on for the rest of the season and Mansell returned to the team.

In the last round of the 1994 Championship in Australia, Hill had sight of the title but was involved in a controversial accident with an up-and-coming German, Michael Schumacher, who took it by one point. Five wins by Hill and a win for Mansell in Australia gave Williams a hat-trick of Constructors' titles. As an unhappy aftermath, Frank Williams and Head faced possible manslaughter charges in Italy arising from Senna's death which were not dismissed for many years.

The F1 capacity limit was reduced to 3.0 litres in 1995, when Renault were supplying engines to Benetton, Schumacher's team, as well as Williams. Mansell had not stayed so David Coulthard was taken on to back up Hill, who won four Championship rounds, while Coulthard scored his first win. The combination of Schumacher and Benetton was too powerful, however, taking both titles.

Schumacher left Benetton for Ferrari in 1996, so Williams was the Renault favourite again. In the annual driver roundabout Coulthard had gone to McLaren and Williams signed Jacques Villeneuve, the son of Gilles, and so had two sons of famous fathers in the team. In the Championship, which became a straight fight between the two Williams drivers, Hill came out on top, winning eight rounds and following his father as a World Champion. Villeneuve was runner-up with four wins so Williams dominated the Constructors' battle.

It was all change at the end of 1996, as Frank Williams decided to dispense with his newly-crowned Champion for 1997; unbeknownst to Damon Hill his representatives were asking for too much money. Newey also departed after a disagreement with Patrick Head. The changes made little difference since Villeneuve was World Champion with seven wins, edging out Schumacher who was disqualified from the Championship for 'avoidable'

accidents. Heinz-Harald Frenzen, who had the second Williams, won at Imola, so Williams took the Constructor's title again – but for the last time. An era had ended.

Another era also ended when the Williams headquarters moved from Didcot to nearby Grove in the late 1990s. In 1998 Williams had a problem when Renault pulled out of the engine deal, so the team had to use Mecachrome engines which were earlier rebuilt Renault units. Rothmans, who had been the sponsor since 1994, changed the cars' livery, so the apparent sponsor was Winfield, a Rothmans brand.

The 1998 season was poor with two third places the best that Frenzen and Villeneuve could manage. Both drivers left at the end of the year and Ralf Schumacher and Alex Zanardi were signed for 1999. A deal had been signed with BMW to supply V-10 engines for the FW21 but these would not come until 2000. Schumacher managed to gain some places but Williams were down in fifth place among the constructors.

BMW took a season to come to terms with F1 again

Nigel Mansell in the Renault-engined 1992 FW14.

Damon Hill with the FW15C in the 1993 European Grand Prix at Donington.

so there were no wins in 2000. Again Michael Schumacher's younger brother Ralf picked up some places while the new boy in the team, Britain's Jenson Button, was finding his feet, like BMW. Button's stay did not last, as for 2001 he was displaced by Juan Pablo Montoya. The year 2001 was a great improvement since Schumacher picked up three wins and Colombian Montoya scored another; so Williams was third among the constructors and BMW had something to show for its input. Williams had abandoned 'politically incorrect' tobacco sponsorship and turned to the IT company, Compaq.

Unfortunately 2001's impetus was not maintained in 2002. Montoya had one win in a season dominated by Ferrari and Michael Schumacher, who had won the Championship with six rounds to go. Although Williams was pursuing in vain, the results did give the team second place in the Constructors' Championship.

Williams was best of the rest again in 2003, the constructors' runner-up behind an uncatchable Ferrari. Montoya won two rounds, as did Ralf Schumacher. Aerodynamic problems slowed the FW26 during the first part of 2004 and the team was disqualified from one round for technical infringements, so not until the last race of the season, in Brazil, was there a win for Montoya. Sadly this was the last F1 victory for Williams at the time of writing.

Tensions increased between Williams and BMW, each blaming the other for the failure to achieve real success and Williams reluctant to accept great involvement in its

Juan Pablo Montoya in the BMW-engined 2002 FW24.

Montoya in the 2004 FW26.

team by the Munich giant. New drivers for 2005 were the Australian Mark Webber and the German Nick Heidfeld, who was compatible with BMW. The results were poor so BMW pulled out to create its own team by buying Sauber in Switzerland.

This left Williams to find a new engine supplier for the changed F1 regulations of 2006. The team turned to Cosworth, who supplied a 2.4-litre V-8. There was a change of driver too, Heidfeld being replaced by Nico Rosberg, the son of Keke, becoming the third father and son to have driven for Williams. It was a bad season with little to show, Williams slipping to an ignominious eighth place among the constructors.

Alexander Wurz replaced Webber in 2007 and the main commercial sponsorship shifted to Allianz, the insurance group, and the Royal Bank of Scotland. More importantly a deal was done with Toyota to supply engines in a season that showed signs of a recovery. There were no wins, but there were some places and the future could be better.

Williams's commitment has been devoted almost exclusively to Formula 1. Among its few non-F1 projects was development of the Rover Metro 6R4 rally car in 1980 and preparation of the successful Renault Laguna for the British Touring Car Championship in the 1990s. Williams also built the V-12 LMR for BMW which was victorious at Le Mans in 1999.

The Williams story has been remarkable. It has been a fight against many adversities, not least for Sir Frank Williams, whose personal courage and achievements were acknowledged when he was knighted in 1999. In recent years the team has been less successful but if any term can be used for Williams, it is indomitable. If past form is a guide, success will surely come again.

CHAPTER 19

McLaren: From Small Acorns...

Bruce McLaren
30 August 1937 – 2 June 1970

BRUCE McLaren arrived in England in 1958 aged 20. He started racing in his native New Zealand with an Austin Seven, then moved on to a sports Cooper. Showing promise he was sent to England on a 'scholarship' by the New Zealand Grand Prix Association.

McLaren hit the ground racing rather than running. He drove a works F2 Cooper in 1958 then joined Jack Brabham in the Cooper F1 team and won his first F1 G.P. in the United States in 1959, to become the youngest-ever G.P. winner. He stayed loyal to Cooper through 1965, like Brabham before him eventually tiring of the Coopers' resistance to new ideas.

In 1964 McLaren raced the Cooper Zerex special, a sports-racing car with an Oldsmobile engine. Encouraged by some success, and not bereft of considerable mechanical aptitude, he founded Bruce McLaren Motor Racing in partnership with the American, Teddy Mayer, in a small works at Colnbrook, near Heathrow Airport.

With ideas of success in the lucrative American market and anticipating the Can-Am series of races, McLaren and Mayer built a sports-racing car, the M1A, firstly with an Oldsmobile engine but later with Chevrolet power. In 1966 McLaren boldly entered F1 with his own car, the M2B, designed by Robin Herd. Initially it had a modified Indy Ford V-8, then a V-8 Serenissima engine. Neither was successful, although McLaren's first Championship point was scored at Brands Hatch with the latter unit. In 1967 BRM and Weslake engines were tried but abandoned. In F2 there was some success with an M4A.

The Herd-designed M7A was built for 1968 with a Ford-Cosworth DFV engine, McLaren having wangled pole position – with Tyrrell and Matra – to use the exciting new V-8 after it lost its Lotus exclusivity. As driver McLaren had been joined by Denny Hulme, the 1967 World Champion and the orange Gulf Oil-sponsored cars had a successful season. McLaren won in Belgium, the first of a run of F1 wins for the marque that has continued for 40 years, while Hulme took the flag in Italy and Canada, giving McLaren the runner-up place in the Constructors' Championship.

Development of the Chevrolet-powered sports-racers continued. The Herd-designed M6A took Bruce McLaren to the 1967 Can-Am Championship, while the following year the M8A dominated the Can-Am series, consolidating a rich source of dollars for the Kiwi team.

McLaren and Hulme raced the M7A in 1969. They gained only one win as the team had spent much on development of an abortive F1 four-wheel-drive car, the

M9A, while Goodyear, on which McLaren was running, was slightly behind in the tyre race. There was compensation as McLaren was the Can-Am Champion again with the M8B and the M10A built for Formula 5000 gained some wins.

When Robin Herd departed to design an abortive four-wheel-drive car for Cosworth and then to found March, Ralph Bellamy picked up his pen, producing the M14A for 1970. Before the season was properly under way the whole McLaren venture almost foundered when Bruce McLaren was killed while testing a Can-Am M8D at Goodwood in June 1970.

Teddy Mayer carried on, but understandably the F1 results were disappointing in spite of the recruitment of Dan Gurney as driver. Hulme again dominated the Can-Am series. It was no better in 1971; Hulme was supported by various drivers and the M19s were mid-field runners. It was a different story in the United States, where the M16, the development of the M10A, was winning in USAC races, and an Offy-powered car driven by Peter Revson was second in the 1971 Indy 500.

Bellamy left at the end of 1971 after disagreements with Mayer. Gordon Coppuck, who had designed the Can-Am and Indy cars, took over the F1 designs. New sponsorship came in 1972 from Yardley, the cosmetics company. The season began well with a Hulme win in South Africa. Several places were gained by Hulme and Revson during the year with the modified M19. The real triumph came at Indianapolis when Mark Donohue won with an Offy-powered M16 prepared and raced by Roger Penske's team.

Coppuck's first F1 design was the M23, for which he drew heavily on the M16. It was a big advance on the M19. In 1973 Hulme won in Sweden and Revson was the winner in Britain and Canada. On the other side of the coin, South African Jody Scheckter spun his M23 on the opening lap at Silverstone and provoked a race-stopping nine-car shunt.

The 1974 season was a big one for McLaren. Marlboro, a brand of the tobacco company Philip Morris, was a new sponsor, while Mayer had lured 1972 World Champion, Emerson Fittipaldi, away from Lotus. Backed by Hulme, Fittipaldi took the Championship again, winning three rounds. These results, combined with a win by Hulme, gave McLaren the Constructors' Championship for the first time. The successes were rounded off by a second win in the Indy 500 where Johnny Rutherford was the victor.

Hulme retired from F1 at the end of 1974 and Fittipaldi could not repeat the success in 1975, as Ferrari

The M2B with Bruce McLaren at the wheel makes its debut at Monaco in 1966.

and Niki Lauda were on a high, though there were two McLaren wins. Fittipaldi left to drive for his own F1 team in 1976, so Mayer signed up James Hunt. Nicknamed 'Hunt the Shunt', the devil-may-care Briton had an erratic record while driving for the enthusiastic but under-funded Hesketh team.

Hunt rewarded Mayer's faith in him by winning the World Championship with a lightened and modified M23, albeit by only one point from Lauda, aided by Lauda's enforced absence after his serious crash in Germany. To complete the success of 1976 Rutherford won again at Indianapolis.

In 1977 the M23 was starting its fifth F1 season and becoming obsolete, so Coppuck produced the honeycomb-chassis M26, which appeared in mid-season and gave Hunt three wins. With ground effects now dominating F1 the M26 was off the pace in 1978, so Coppuck produced his own ground-effect car for 1979, the M28, but as a contemporary writer commented, McLaren were 'entering a long, dark tunnel'. The M28, and the M29 built for the 1980 season, produced dismal results.

Marlboro had been sponsoring an F2 team, Project 4, which was run by Ron Dennis who had entered motor racing in 1966 as a mechanic for the Cooper team. Concerned at the poor McLaren results, Marlboro

Mark Donohue in the M16 which won the 1972 Indianapolis 500.

McLaren in the M7A during the Race of Champions at Brands Hatch in 1969.

The M16E which took Johnny Rutherford to victory in the 1976 Indianapolis 500.

JAMES HUNT

Born near Sutton in Surrey in 1947, James Hunt was destined to become a controversial and colourful World Champion. He began racing a Mini then moved on to Formula Ford in 1968. A step up to F3 soon followed with Hunt building a reputation as a wild and erratic driver: 'Hunt the Shunt'.

In 1972, when Hunt joined Lord Hesketh's F2 team driving a March, his driving matured rapidly. In 1973 Hesketh moved into F1 with a March and Hunt, moving with him, picked up several impressive places, missing victory in the United States G.P. by less than a second.

Hesketh developed his own F1 car, a typical Cosworth-powered 'British kit car'. Hunt raced this in 1974 and 1975, picking up some places and scoring the only win for the Hesketh team in the 1975 Dutch G.P. When Hesketh gave up, McLaren's Teddy Mayer recognised his talent and signed Hunt for his team in 1976. His faith was rewarded and

Hunt became World Champion, winning six rounds.

The McLaren M26, introduced halfway through the 1977 season, gave Hunt three wins, but the Japanese G.P. at the end of the season would be his last F1 victory. With the McLaren team having technical problems, 1978 was a lean year for Hunt so he moved to the Wolf F1 team in 1979, when his results were even more dismal.

James Hunt seemed to have lost motivation and retired from the sport halfway through the 1979 season. In retirement Hunt became a TV commentator for the BBC on F1 races, forming a celebrated duo with Murray Walker. Both the motor racing world and a wider public, aware of Hunt's off-track adventures as reported by the tabloids, were shocked when the former driver died of a heart attack in 1993, aged only 46.

James Hunt in the M23 at Monaco in 1977.

The McLaren F1GTR of Andy Wallace and Olivier Grouillard winning the 1995 Silverstone Four-Hours.

dominated the Constructors' rankings by a margin of 83 points.

In 1985 Prost was not to be denied. He took the title while McLaren was the Constructors' Champion for the second year. In 1986 Prost won the crown again, though Williams pipped McLaren in the constructors' race. The TAG engine was becoming less competitive by 1987, though Prost scored three wins.

After John Barnard left to join Ferrari at the end of 1986, McLaren design was taken over by Steve Nichols and Gordon Murray, who had come from Brabham. The complexity of Formula 1 design was now such that it was the responsibility of a specialist team rather than individuals. Profiting by tensions between Williams and Honda, Dennis secured the Honda V-6 engine for 1988, a deal aided by also acquiring the services of Ayrton Senna, who had been supported by Honda when driving for Team Lotus.

brokered Mayer and McLaren into an amalgamation with Project 4 to form McLaren International.

The conflation brought big changes. Coppuck departed and was replaced by John Barnard, who had worked with Coppuck on the M23 from 1972 to 1975. McLaren moved from Colnbrook into a new factory at Woking. Barnard designed the MP4/1 – with Lotus the first to use a carbon-fibre tub – which scored its first F1 win at Silverstone in 1981 driven by John Watson. Then Dennis bought out Mayer to take control of McLaren.

In 1982 Lauda joined the team. He and Watson scored two wins each, but the DFV Cosworth was being surpassed by the turbos, so Dennis replaced it with a V-6 designed and built by Porsche. This TAG turbo V-6 was funded by Mansour Ojjeh who had previously been a sponsor of the Williams F1 team and became a major shareholder in McLaren.

After a slow start in 1983 the TAG-engined MP4/2 dominated the 1984 season. Lauda was Champion, beating Alain Prost, in the other McLaren seat, by the impossibly narrow margin of half a point. McLaren

In 1988 the combination of Senna, Prost, Honda and McLaren was formidable. Every race bar one was won by the McLaren drivers, McLaren winning the Constructors' title by the huge margin of 134 points from Ferrari, while Senna was World Champion. The problem of having two champions in the team came to a head in 1989 when the pair fought it out using the Honda V-10 engine in the MP4/5. After a controversial collision in Japan, Prost seized the title, with their joint successes making McLaren the top constructor again.

In 1990 Prost went to Ferrari, leaving Senna a clear run to the Championship in the MP4/5B, his efforts taking McLaren to a hat-trick of Constructors' titles – though the season ended with another Senna/Prost collision. It was the same Senna/McLaren success story in 1991. The pairing of Renault with Williams displaced Honda and McLaren from the top spot in 1992, though Senna won three F1 rounds.

Thereafter Ron Dennis suffered a major set-back when Honda pulled out. For 1993 he had to rely on a

1999 McLaren MP4/14-Mercedes

The McLaren MP4/14 which took Mika Häkkinen to a second World Championship in 1999. Sponsored by tobacco manufacturer West and powered by the Mercedes-Ilmor engine, the MP4/14 won five races for Häkkinen and another two for his team-mate, David Coulthard. Despite the Mercedes connection, it was an all-British success as the car was built at Woking, Surrey and the engine at Brixworth, Northamptonshire.

The disappointing McLaren-Mercedes MP4/10 of 1995.

Ford V-8 with which Senna picked up four wins. The going was getting harder. In 1994 the MP4/9, designed by Neil Oatley, used a Peugeot V-10, whose principal merit was that it was free. The racing produced minimal dividends.

Mercedes-Benz, one of the truly great names in motor racing, had not competed in F1 since 1955, but since the late 1980s it had been weighing various paths back to the top level of motor sport. In 1995 Mercedes-Benz entered into a partnership with McLaren to supply engines. The engines do not originate in Stuttgart but are made at Brixworth, in England's 'Carburettor Valley', by Mercedes-Benz High Performance Engines. This was formerly Ilmor Engineering, an independent company which was commissioned to produce a 3.5-litre V-10 engine for the F1 McLaren.

There were no great results in 1995 and '96, but in 1997 Adrian Newey was lured from Williams to join the Woking design team. His influence was immediate. Using the MP4/12, David Coulthard won two F1 rounds and another went to Mika Häkkinen. There was also a new backer with West, a Rothmans cigarette brand, replacing long-time sponsor Marlboro.

It all came good for Häkkinen in 1998. The Finn won eight Championship rounds to become Champion while Coulthard backed up well and won a round; so McLaren were Constructors' Champions again. Häkkinen did it again in 1999, though his task was made easier when his biggest rival, Michael Schumacher on Ferrari, missed seven rounds while recovering from an accident.

Although the Schumacher show was back on the road in 2000, winning the Drivers' crown, Häkkinen and Coulthard did well, winning eight Championship rounds between them and securing the runner-up place for McLaren in the constructors' title. It was the same story in 2001; Schumacher was relentless and Coulthard and Häkkinen could only pick up crumbs, but McLaren was the runner-up again.

Häkkinen retired from Formula 1 at the end of 2001 and his McLaren seat was taken by another Finn, Kimi Räikkonen, but the going had become harder. Coulthard could gain only one victory for the team. The MP4/18 introduced for 2003 was unsatisfactory and so the team had to use the MP4/17D raced the previous year. Despite this set-back Räikkonen found his form in 2003, gaining one win and a string of seconds behind Schumacher to become Championship runner-up.

The MP4/19 produced by Newey for 2004 had aerodynamic problems and was revised to become the MP4/19B in mid-season. Although it was more competitive, Räikkonen and Coulthard could do nothing to stop Schumacher who won 13 of the 18 Championship rounds.

Mercedes-Benz took control of Ilmor in 2005. At McLaren, Juan Pablo Montoya replaced Coulthard, scoring three wins, while Räikkonen was chasing Fernando Alonso for the Championship. After a hesitant start to the season he took seven rounds to be runner-up while the chase for the Constructors' title was also close, with Renault just heading off McLaren.

The change in F1 regulations for 2006 saw the introduction of a Mercedes 2.4-litre V-8 while the McLarens appeared in a new silver and black livery that emphasised the Mercedes connection. A lack of reliability, power and general form – perhaps a consequence of the departure of Newey – left the McLarens trailing behind the Renaults and Ferraris and shut out of victories.

Montoya walked out after a disagreement at the end of the season and Räikkonen was poached by Ferrari, so it was all change for 2007, including sponsorship. An EU ban on tobacco advertising saw the departure of West, so a deal was signed with Vodafone, who were poached from Ferrari. Dennis signed double-Champion Alonso and gave the second seat to Briton Lewis Hamilton, who had been nurtured by McLaren since his boyhood karting debut.

An unheralded rivalry between the experienced Alonso and novice Hamilton saw an intense season where both drivers fought each other and Räikkonen. Only a point separated the three at the end, with the Ferrari driver on top. Allegations that industrial espionage, involving the use of Ferrari secrets, had benefited McLaren saw the team stripped of its Constructors' title points by the FIA.

Away from Grand Prix racing McLaren developed the F1 road car with a BMW V-12 engine. In the 1990s and in GTR competition form this gained many successes, most notably victory at Le Mans in 1995 with GTRs also taking 3rd, 4th and 5th places.

Despite its long-lasting Mercedes-Benz connection, McLaren is as much an all-British team as any of the great marques that carried BRG in the past. Much of its success for over 25 years is due to the single-minded dedication of Ron Dennis, whose achievements received official recognition when he was appointed a CBE in 1999. Although always looking to the future, McLaren remains proud of its roots in the feisty, questing Bruce McLaren, who began his career in the green Coopers of Surbiton.

Lewis Hamilton receives the plaudits of the crowd after winning the 2007 Canadian Grand Prix in his MP4/22.

CHAPTER 20

The Rest: Minor Triumphs, Noble Failures

The first British Grand Prix contender. Harrison's Weigel in the 1907 French Grand Prix.

Ron Godfrey at the wheel of Archie Frazer-Nash's sprint GN 'Mowgli' in the GN works at Battersea in 1921.

DURING the last century many British teams and marques have achieved triumphs in motoring competition that have made them household names. In the preceding chapters their exploits have been revered and praised. Others, however, have toiled to achieve minor successes or failed through ill-fortune, lack of funds, mismanagement or some combination of these. Their feats and failures are now largely forgotten, but they too wore British Racing Green and carried the flag in the hope of success.

When the Gordon Bennett races were abandoned in 1905, the Automobile Club de France stepped in and founded the Grand Prix de l'ACF in 1906, better known as the French Grand Prix. There were no British entries in the 1906 race, but a year later the first British Grand Prix car appeared in the lists.

Danny Weigel was the managing director of Clement Talbot, an early British manufacturer. In 1906 he started making cars bearing his own name in a small factory in London. His production cars, which were only made in small numbers, owed much to Italy's contemporary Itala, but it seems that much of the manufacture was undertaken by other companies and the cars were only assembled in Weigel's small works. The chassis frames were made by Wilkinsons, now better known for razor blades.

The first Weigel had a 7.4-litre four-cylinder engine. Realising the value of motor racing to publicise his new company, Weigel built two cars for the 1907 French G.P. These had straight-eight engines which were in effect two of his 7.4-litre four-cylinder units coupled together. The resulting engine was long, with an over-flexible crankcase, and drove through a two-speed gearbox.

The Grand Prix was held in July 1907 over 10 laps of a 47-mile circuit outside Dieppe. The Weigels, driven by Gregor Laxen and Pryce Harrison, were outclassed by most of the field. Laxen made several stops on the first lap to change tyres and retired after three laps, while Harrison did a little better and lasted for six laps. At the end of July 1907 the Weigels were taken to Belgium for the Circuit des Ardennes where they finished the course albeit a lap behind and at the tail of the field.

Weigel built three new cars for the 1908 French G.P, held again on the Dieppe road circuit. These had four-cylinder engines of 12.7 litres and three-speed gearboxes. The cars were too heavy, 600 pounds (277 kg) more than the winning Mercedes. Drivers Harrison and Laxen and new man Shannon had no better fortune than in 1907. Shannon retired after two laps with defective steering, Laxen hit a tree and Harrison went off the road and overturned, fortunately without injury. That was the end of the racing ventures of Weigel, which went into receivership in 1909.

Soon after Weigel left Clement Talbot, the latter London-based company entered motor sport. The 4½-litre 25 hp Talbot became a regular competitor when Brooklands opened in 1907. A special single-seater was developed with a narrow body. With this car Percy Lambert took the World hour record at Brooklands in February 1913, becoming the first to cover 100 miles in the hour. Unfortunately Lambert was killed in November 1913 while attempting a new hour record.

In 1919 Talbot became a part of the Sunbeam-Talbot-Darracq combine (see Chapter 3) and was joined by Georges Roesch, a brilliant Swiss designer who developed a range of high-performance pushrod engines. A team of Roesch's 2.3-litre Talbot 90s, supported by the factory, was raced in 1930 by Fox & Nicoll, a motor firm at Tolworth on the route from London to Brooklands.

After a disastrous debut when one of the cars crashed into the crowd during the 1930 Double-Twelve at Brooklands, killing a spectator, the 90s showed excellent form and gained several places including a third at Le Mans, also winning the Index of Performance. For 1931 Roesch produced the 3.0-litre 105 Talbot which came third at Le Mans in 1931 and 1932 and gained places in many other events,

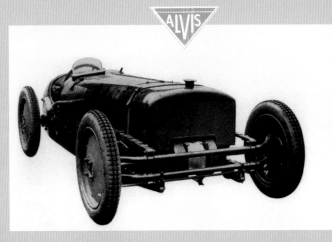

although an outright win just eluded the Fox & Nicoll Talbot team.

In rallying the 105 achieved great success in the Alpine Trial, but financial stringencies curtailed Talbot racing. Fox & Nicoll transferred their interest to Lagonda. After 1935, when the Sunbeam-Talbot-Darracq combine became part of the Rootes group, Talbot's racing days were over. In 1981, when Peugeot-Citröen were reviving the Talbot brand, Ligier's F1 cars ran as 'Talbot Ligiers', exploiting past awareness of the marque in both Britain and France.

When the Alvis company emerged in Coventry just after World War One, it began producing a range of sporting cars. The 12/50 Alvis was introduced in 1923. A 12/50, mildly modified and tuned, gained fame as the unexpected winner of the 1923 JCC 200-mile race at Brooklands. The 12/50 continued to find success, sports models winning the Essex Six-Hour race on handicap, and the JCC Four-Hour Sporting Car race at Brooklands in 1927.

Alvis was a European pioneer of front-wheel drive. The company's designer, W. M. Dunn, produced a 1.5-litre front-drive car which ran in the 1925 JCC 200-mile race. With immense ambition in 1926 a front-drive Grand Prix car was built with an eight-cylinder engine. This 1½-litre car raced twice in 1926 and 1927 but without success. However a four-cylinder front-drive sports Alvis ran at Le Mans in 1928, winning the 1.5-litre class, and came second in the Ulster Tourist Trophy. In fact it has been alleged that the Alvis won the TT but was denied victory by a lap-scoring error.

The eight-cylinder Grand Prix engine went into the front-drive sports Alvis in 1930 and gained a class win in the TT. After that Alvis left racing to private owners, who gained many successes at Brooklands and other venues in the years up to World War Two. Thereafter Alvis cars, although meritorious, were not marked by sporting ambitions.

It was a Lea-Francis that denied Alvis the 1928 TT victory. Founded by Richard Lea and Graham Francis, Lea-Francis – initially Lea & Francis – began making bicycles in Coventry in the 19th century. Car manufacture began in the early 1920s. A sports car, the Hyper model, with a supercharged 1.5-litre Meadows engine, appeared in 1928. The Hyper gained a number of class wins but the TT was its only major victory.

While the factory did not return to racing, private owners raced the Hyper into the 1930s. After World War Two Lea-Francis produced a four-cylinder engine with twin high camshafts and hemispherical chambers on Riley lines. A derivative of this intended for American midget racing became the basis of the power unit of the A-type Connaught (see page 74).

At the beginning of the 20th century some auto makers sought to meet low-cost demand with small-capacity, lightweight cars dubbed 'cycle-cars'. The term embraced three-wheelers and small four-wheeled cars under 1.1 litre capacity. By 1913 these became very popular. England had a flourishing Cyclecar Club and the first cyclecar race had been held at Brooklands in 1912 and won by a Morgan.

The ACF recognised the popularity of the class, in 1913 organising the G.P. de l'ACF des Cyclecars, held at Amiens on the same circuit as the French G.P. on the day following the Grand Prix. A field of 30 included a team of four Morgans. One of these, driven by William McMinnies, won the race, only to be disqualified. The organisers declared after the race that three-wheelers were ineligible and so the victory was awarded to a French Bedelia.

Controversy raged over such a seemingly chauvinistic decision. In England the Morgan was regarded as the winner of this inaugural race. To confuse the issue the ACF presented McMinnies with a commemorative gold medal. This was the only major international 'victory' gained by the three-wheel Morgan, although the cars gained countless awards in trials and at Brooklands.

Eventually the Morgan grew up into the four-wheeled 4/4, Plus 4 and Plus 8 sports cars. The Plus 4 gained class successes at Le Mans, Nürburgring, Sebring and other venues in the 1960s – often a proud wearer of the green. In the 21st century Morgan continues to evolve racing versions of its classically styled sports cars.

The 1926 front-wheel drive Grand Prix Alvis.

The Lea-Francis team lines up before the 1928 Ulster Tourist Trophy.

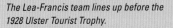

TALBOT

The team of 1931 Talbot 105s at Brooklands.

The Le Mans Replica Frazer Nash which won the 1951 Targa Florio.

FRAZER NASH

dog-engagement transmission, these became popular and successful competition cars for the amateur driver, though they had a reputation for unreliability in longer races. In 1929 the motor-trading Aldington brothers acquired the Frazer Nash company and continued to build more refined versions into the mid-1930s. The reputation for unreliability in longer races remained, though there were most impressive performances in the Alpine Trials.

In the years before World War Two, the Aldingtons became the British agent for BMW, including the advanced 328 sports car. Immediately after the war they were instrumental in obtaining the 328 engine design for the Bristol Aeroplane Company, which enabled Bristol to produce their own range of cars, showing a strong affinity with the pre-war BMW.

At their small works at Isleworth in London's south-west reaches the Aldingtons began producing a range of Frazer Nash sports cars using the Bristol engine, gearbox and other parts. One of these took third place in the first post-war Le Mans race in 1949. In 1951 a Le Mans Replica Frazer Nash, driven by the Italian Franco Cortese, achieved a remarkable feat by winning the demanding Targa Florio in Sicily, the only time this tough race was ever won by a British car. A Le Mans Replica was the winner on distance of the first Sebring 12-hour race in 1952, driven by Larry Kulok and Harry Grey.

In the early 1950s the light and lively Frazer Nash was a formidable competitor in the 2.0-litre class in long-distance sports car events, scoring many wins. As well, three single-seat Formula 2 versions were built for the 1952 season. Only one, a green car in Ken Wharton's hands, gained an international profile with a fourth place in the 1952 Swiss G.P. After an abortive BMW V-8-powered effort the Aldingtons, having discovered the pleasure of importing and selling Porsches, ceased producing Frazer Nashes in 1958.

Motorcycle racing in the 1920s by his grandfather and great uncle was in the bloodline of Adrian Reynard. Born in 1951, Reynard saw his first race at Silverstone at the age of eight. Starting as a motorcycle sprinter, in 1973 he began making chassis for Formula Ford, a popular entry-level class for motor racing aspirants. By 1975 Reynard was ensconced in premises at Bicester, not far from March.

Reynard's design soon dominated Formula Ford. By the time that class was phased out 661 Reynards had been built to suit it. The company moved on to Formula 3 in the 1980s and again enjoyed great success. A Formula 3000 design which appeared in the late 1980s saw Reynard ruling that formula too. F3000 was especially popular in Japan, where many of the 220 cars made were raced.

It was a logical move from F3000 to the CART class in the United States, which Reynard entered in 1994. There was almost immediate success with Jacques Villeneuve winning the

Competing against the Morgans at Amiens were two GNs. This cyclecar was built by Archie Frazer-Nash and Ron Godfrey in a former laundry in the North London suburb of Hendon. It was unkindly alleged that metal components from the old laundry equipment found their way into the early GNs. Although the two cars had no success at Amiens, by 1914 the GN, with its air-cooled vee-twin engine, had built a big reputation as a nimble, fast road car as well as a successful competition car in British events.

After World War One this reputation flourished. A GN was a class winner in the first 200-mile race at Brooklands in 1921. The GN was built in France under licence as the Salmson, a make which later grew into a most successful competition car of the 1920s.

Economic forces and the arrival of the Austin Seven killed off the GN, so Archie Frazer-Nash began building cars under his own name in the 1920s – albeit usually non-hyphenated. With their unique multiple-chain and

Jacques Villeneuve and his team with the Reynard which won the 1995 Indianapolis 500.

Thrust SSC.

1995 Indy 500 in a Reynard powered by a Cosworth DFX engine. There was an Indy victory again in 1996 when the winner was Buddy Lazier in a Reynard-Cosworth. Reynard dominated the CART series, providing the champion's mount for four successive years. An attempt to enter F1 was less successful and the project was abandoned in 1992.

Success in the United States resulted in the purchase of the American Riley & Scott company, which made sports-racing cars, but financial problems forced Reynard into liquidation in 2002 and the factory, by then situated at Brackley, was closed. Adrian Reynard continues to work as an automotive consultant. The success of Reynard was recognised when his company received the Queen's Award for Export Achievement in 1990 and 1996.

Thanks to the single-minded devotion and dedication of one man, Richard Noble, Britain enjoyed success in record-breaking which recalled the great days of Segrave, Campbell, Eyston and Cobb. Setting out to regain the Land Speed Record for Britain, Noble found sponsorship for a car designed by John Ackroyd. It was propelled by a Rolls-Royce Avon jet engine that had formerly powered an RAF Lightning fighter. Driven by Noble, Thrust 2 took the record at Black Rock Desert in Nevada in October 1983, achieving 633.88 mph.

Richard Noble wanted to build the first supersonic record-breaker. Working with Glynne Bowsher, Ron Ayres and Jeremy Bliss a new car, Thrust SSC, was designed and built using two Rolls-Royce Spey jet engines. In October 1997 Thrust SSC was taken to Black Rock Desert where, driven by RAF Squadron Leader Andy Green, it went supersonic by raising the record to 763.035 mph. Fittingly Thrust SSC was painted dark green. Thus it was truly in the great tradition of earlier generations of British cars which had held this coveted record.

Many other names should be remembered in a panorama of the wearers of the green. Among them are AC and Allard, both winners of the Monte Carlo Rally, Austin-Healey, Elva, Healey, HRG, Invicta – another Monte winner – Jowett, Kieft, Lister, Singer, Squire, Triumph, Turner, TVR and more. Only the major players have qualified to be in this book, but the others all strove mightily.

Some failed and sank without trace. Others came up with a successful design which achieved short-term success, but then foundered. So often the lack of funds has been a vital factor, but the qualities of enthusiasm and engineering expertise have never been in short supply. All deserve praise as they bravely wore the green.

Bibliography

Allison, Mike & Browning, Peter: *The Works MGs* (Haynes 2000).

Berthon, Darell: *The Racing History of the Bentley* (Autobooks 1962)

Blight, Anthony; *Georges Roesch and the Invincible Talbot* (Grenville Publishing 1970)

Boddy, William: *Brooklands – The Complete Motor Racing History* (MRP Publishing 2001)

Davey, Arnold & May, Anthony: *Lagonda – A History of the Marque* (David & Charles 1978)

Georgano, Nick (Ed): *The Encyclopaedia of Motor Sport* (Ebury Press & Michael Joseph 1971)

—— *The Beaulieu Encyclopaedia of the Automobile* (The Stationery Office 2000)

Harrison, Roland. C: *Austin Racing History:* (Motor Racing Publications 1949)

Heal, Anthony: *Sunbeam Racing Cars* (Haynes 1989)

Henry, Alan: *Brabham – The Grand Prix Cars* (Hazelton Publishing 1989)

—— *March – The Grand Prix & Indy Cars* (Hazelton Publishing 1989)

Hull, Peter & Johnson, Norman: *The Vintage Alvis* (The Alvis Register 1995)

Hunter, Inman: *Aston Martin 1913-1947* (Osprey 1992)

Jenkinson, Denis: *Directory of Historic Racing Cars* (Aston Publications 1987)

Jenkinson, Denis & Posthumus, Cyril: *Vanwall* (Patrick Stephens 1975)

Ludvigsen, Karl: *Stirling Moss* (Haynes 1997)

Mathieson, T.A.S.O: *Grand Prix Racing 1906-1914* (Connoisseur Automobile 1965)

Nye, Doug: *Cooper Cars* (Osprey 1983)

—— *History of the Grand Prix Car 1945-65* (Hazelton Publishing 1993)

—— *History of the Grand Prix Car 1966-91* (Hazelton Publishing 1992)

Popely, Rick: *Indianapolis 500 Chronicle* (Publications International 1998)

Rose, Gerald: *A Record of Motor Racing 1894-1908* (Motor Racing Publications 1949)

Sheldon, Paul & Rabagliati, Duncan: *A Record of Grand Prix & Voiturette Racing* – Volumes 8-13 (St Leonards Press 1994-2002)

Small, Steve: *Grand Prix Who's Who* (Guinness Publishing 1996)

Styles, David: *Sporting Rileys – The Forgotten Champions* (Dalton Watson 1988)

Venables, David: *Napier – The First to Wear the Green* (Haynes 1998)

—— *Brooklands – The Official Centenary History* (Haynes 2007)

Weguelin, David: *ERA – The History of English Racing Automobiles* (White Mouse Editions 1980)

Whyte, Andrew: *Jaguar Sport Racing Works and Competition Cars to 1953* (Haynes 1982)

—— *Jaguar Sports Racing Works and Competition Cars from 1954* (Haynes 1987)

Wimpffen, János: *Time and Two Seats – Five Decades of Long Distance Racing* (Motor Sport Research Group 1999)

Index